GET YO' LIFE

BLACK PERFORMANCE AND CULTURAL CRITICISM
E. Patrick Johnson, Series Editor

GET YO' LIFE

BLACK QUEER PLACEMAKING

R. J. Millhouse

THE OHIO STATE UNIVERSITY PRESS
COLUMBUS

Library of Congress Cataloging-in-Publication Data
Names: Millhouse, R. J., author.
Title: Get yo' life : Black queer placemaking / R. J. Millhouse.
Other titles: Black performance and cultural criticism.
Description: Columbus : The Ohio State University Press, [2025] | Series: Black performance
    and cultural criticism | Includes bibliographical references and index. | Summary: "Via
    ethnographic case studies of two Brooklyn nightclubs threatened by gentrification,
    introduces Black queer spatiality as both a method for examining what Black queer
    people do and a theory for explaining a Black queer sense of place"—Provided by
    publisher.
Identifiers: LCCN 2024057140 | ISBN 9780814215845 (hardback) | ISBN 081421584X
    (hardback) | ISBN 9780814284070 (ebook) | ISBN 0814284078 (ebook)
Subjects: LCSH: African American gay people—New York (State)—New York—Social
    conditions—Case studies. | Sociology, Urban—New York (State)—New York—
    Case studies. | Spatial behavior—New York (State)—New York—Case studies. |
    Communities—New York (State)—New York—Case studies.
Classification: LCC HQ76.27.A37 M55 2025 | DDC 306.76/608996073—dc23/eng/20241206
LC record available at https://lccn.loc.gov/2024057140

Other identifiers: ISBN 9780814259405 (paperback) | ISBN 0814259405 (paperback)

Cover design by adam bohannon
Text design by Juliet Williams
Type set in Adobe Minion Pro

CONTENTS

ILLUSTRATIONS

ACKNOWLEDGMENTS

Get Yo' Life: Black Queer Placemaking emerges from years of dialogue about Black queer experiences of urban spatial loss, resiliency, and sociospatial (re)production. The dialogue was almost always framed by myriad memories sited in and across a few vanished Black queer spaces. Through conversations with Black queer Brooklynites, archival research, and ethnographies, a slate of mostly spatial memories involves a vanished Black queer space—the sites where Black queer people define, organize, and *do* Black queer public culture. Although the research process was demanding and at times tested the limits of my own resiliency, *Get Yo' Life* focuses on marked, vanished spaces to discuss the extent to which they serve as a mechanism for Black queer people to forge their own personhoods. *Get Yo' Life* would not be possible without my interlocutors. who shared their time, energy, and life experiences with me. I can only dream of accurately articulating, through words only, the level of gratitude that I have for your transparency and trusting me with your stories.

To my cousin Kisha Odom, I am grateful for your consistent check-ins with me from afar through FaceTime messages, family recipes, and family photos. It is because of you that I have photos of my dad and know my paternal family. I remember you gave me a photo album at our family reunion in Birmingham, Alabama. We looked at every page, and you had a story for each photo, or at least I thought so. The album had pictures of Granny, Granddaddy, your mama, my dad, my mama, and our cousins. I also have a photo of your late mother, Shirley, my late mother's friend. Once we reached the middle of the album, our tears flowed faster and our laughter grew louder. I can remember visiting your mama and eating at least three different cakes that she baked. Her German chocolate cake is unmatched. I also remember our mothers would sit with each other, drink coffee, and reminisce about us. They would laugh and giggle after almost every sentence. Thank you, Kisha, for constantly surrounding me with love.

On June 1, 2022, my mother transitioned to another world, suddenly. She was fifty-four years old. Her last words to me were, "Happy June."

I wrote *Get Yo' Life* while on my healing journey. At times, it was difficult to write on spatial loss, anti-Blackness, and spatial and economic challenges while managing my personal grief. To charge myself to write, I would often think about the time I danced with my mom in a lounge in Prichard, Alabama. I would think about how much fun we had that night. We were the only two people on the dance floor and all eyes were on us as we danced. After we left and started walking to her car, I remember her bright smile piercing the night sky. As we got into the car, she laughed and said, "Whew, boy, I haven't danced like since way back!" This memory comforted me while I completed this book.

I am thankful to my friends who supported me through my grief I carried from my mother's transition. My mother's transition impacted me in ways that left me broken, confused, angry, and doubtful. Yet my friends helped me pick up the pieces of my life that I thought I'd lost forever. You helped me get out of my own way, gave me endless words of encouragement, provided space and opportunities for me to laugh, cry, and dream. Your unwavering support has meant everything to me as we spent many days and nights speaking about this project and life that was happening to us. Our conversations would sometimes start with cries and end in laughter, and other times, vice versa. It is because of you that *Get Yo' Life* is out in the world. I appreciate you all beyond measure.

INTRODUCTION

This study investigates queer blackness and its articulations in space. As a paradigm and epistemology, queer Blackness is embodied and is therefore a lived experience informed by discursive constructions which have been influenced by racism. Indeed, queer Blackness has been and remains both the nucleus of global cultures and a site where axes of oppression linger. Historically, Black queer people and their social spaces have consistently been squeezed out of the built environment over time due to anti-Blackness, socio-economic deprivation, and spatial segregation. Therefore, Black queer people must themselves produce places and conditions that support their livelihoods. My project considers uneven development, gentrification, and displacement as spatial forms of bodily control rooted in heteropatriarchy (A. Smith 2010), settler colonialism (Arvin et al. 2013), and white supremacy (A. Smith 2010). Amid these oppressive forces, I locate Black queer spatiality and attend to spatial articulations (McGlotten et al. 2009) that characterize Black queer space, such as bodily sensations, atmospheres, and nostalgia (Farrar 2011; McGlotten 2014). Black queer spatiality not only identifies *what* Black queer people do, but *why* they do what they do. I define Black queer spaces as worlds produced by Black queer people to convene, see themselves outside heteropatriarchy, and live freely.

Black queer spatiality incorporates im/materiality: objects, performances, time, sensations, atmospheres, and nostalgia are all spatial articulations fundamental to spatial re/production that condition social relationships. Spatial articulations are meanings relative to experience, social relationships to other people and power, and desires that are tethered to a particular place and time by people. Spatial articulations also form a queer language of penalty, privilege, and futurity. Shaka McGlotten (2014) discusses spatial dis/articulations inside queer spaces by demonstrating how affect animates, makes sense of, and gives meaning to queer spaces due to the inherent qualities of queer spaces: radical imagination, performance, and production. McGlotten (2012, 46) asks, "What if speculation helped us to think about the many material ways Blackness and queerness are epistemologically and ontologically tied through the particular ways they are simultaneously open and constrained, sensed, and worlded, zones of indeterminacy?" Although this question is hypothetical, it provides an entry point to consider what is gained when we use Black queer spatiality to think about material and immaterial ways Blackness and queerness are spatialized to support the lives of Black queer people particularly.

Methodological Possibilities

The possibilities that Black queer spatiality allows social policy and academic circles include prioritizing the interplay between race, class, gender, sexuality, and space such that land-use policies begin to support Black queer spatial agency and representation.

Black LGBTQ club spaces, for example, are not fixed; they are produced by communal performance and interior interactions within club spaces, including dance, interpersonal interactions, symbolic objects, and sonic rhythms. In this study, I explore the ways in which Black people have produced Black queer community formations at several locations, but primarily at Club Langston and Happiness Lounge, two Brooklyn clubs at which I performed field work from April 2018 to April 2020. I argue that race, class, gender, and sexuality exist in space and manifest through Black queer performances and interactions. As a result of performances and interactions, a Black queer sense of place is produced.

Furthermore, race, class, gender, and sexuality bear histories that have shaped the way people understand their intersections with structures of power. I contend that space is a vector of power that is made clear through spatial articulations of race and gender. Historical and current processes necessitate space for Black queer people in urban areas, such as Brooklyn, New York. These processes condition spatial articulations, and I argue that a more comprehensive theory and method to understand the extent to which they are unique is required. I propose Black queer spatiality to expand the epistemic and ontological dimensions of spatial articulations. Black queer spatiality, moreover, theorizes spatial articulations through observation, questioning, and sensing spatial articulations.

I define "queer" as a performance that disrupts societal norms, disarticulates representations, and finds new, shifting, and unstable ways to imagine how these disruptions and disarticulations fit together (Browne and Nash 2010). Black queer spatiality as a theory maps materiality from spatial production, maintenance, and performance while also recognizing the critical involvement that immateriality has on space and people. By doing so, Black queer spatiality as a theory thinks through how, why, and to what extent space is commodified, policed, multidimensional, and produced as an extension of people relative to its social dimensions and characteristics. As a method, Black queer spatiality maps objects within space to spatial performances and their inherent felt experience. In this regard, Black queer spatiality is a type of memory work that utilizes intersectionality to understand the connection that space has to people's lived realities. For example, why do we feel a certain longing in particular spaces and not others? Black queer spatiality calls attention to atmosphere, nostalgia, and individual and collective sensations that condition Black queer people's spatial experiences within and outside spaces. Black queer spatiality, then, is a larger analytic of space-making and Black LGBTQ public culture that is applied at various scales.

Chapter 1: Black Queer Placemaking

In the first chapter, I demonstrate how dominant, public places can isolate Black queer people while Black queer placemaking may heal and reaffirm them. I argue that place emerges through performance, including the singular gestures of official marking. By official marking, I mean the act of labeling a place or marking a place using written text, such as in the case of renaming a street in Brooklyn "Do The Right Thing Way," a public process I discuss in chapter 1. However, marking place also includes bodily acts, which are almost always coded with geopolitical meanings. For example, at a Do the Right Thing block party, one of the scenes chapter 1 brings to life, I center Aaron's *Snap!* performance at the margins of the gathering to explore Black queer placemaking practice. I focus heavily on a sense of balance, the creation of a bounded place, and spatial imaginary. Aaron's sense of balance is demonstrated by the way he dances and by his crisp finger snaps, which are directed toward the dancing crowd at the block party. Moreover, Aaron's snaps create a boundary or bounded place around the immediate area where he stands on the margins of the crowd. *Snap! Snap! Snap!* The sound of his snaps cuts the sound of the music playing at the block party and his hips move from side to side on beat to the music. His spatial imaginary is acknowledged as he exclaims his sexual desire for one of the Black cisgender male partygoers.

Atmosphere, Nostalgia, and Sensation

Chapter 1 introduces the frameworks of atmosphere, nostalgia, and sensation to investigate how and to what extent place is healing for Black queer people. I argue that atmospheres (Anderson 2009; Funes 1998; McHugh 2009) have both subjective and objective qualities that are felt (emotional) and pre-personal (affective). I discuss atmosphere as the object of inquiry waiting to be discovered through its im/materially emotive and affective capabilities by reflecting on a FaceTime conversation with Aaron textured by the R&B music that played loudly during our conversation. On the one hand, atmospheres become through the happenings within their indeterminate boundaries. On the other hand, atmospheres become through what bodies or things do along the boundaries of the atmospheric envelope.

Nostalgia is realized when bodies are oriented in a certain direction, especially under conditions of the horizon: time of day, social interactions, and displacement. Nostalgia, then, is a yearning or longing for a certain place-time. Nostalgia, according to Jennifer Kitson and Kevin McHugh (2015, 490), "is a lively, pre-personal affect which registers in and through the sensory contact of bodies and things." I center the 1990s R&B music that textured my phone conversation with Aaron to demonstrate nostalgia's affect through the interface of our cell phones. Lastly, I discuss spatial articulations as a humanistic social scientific concept that identifies marked elements, spatial interactions, and sensations that are unique to a particular place and time; spatial articulations describe a sense of place, in part. Inside Langston's, as I show in chapter 1, spatial articulations are recognized in the club's materialisms: the music playlist, the posters on the walls, the musky smell of the space, the selection of drinks that are available, and the objects and materials found across the bar.

Following the contestations of Kitson and McHugh (2015), "things" that are both seen and unseen have intensities and aesthetic capacities, as they are objects that I am "orientated" toward (Ahmed 2008). Since my gaze is orientated toward these "things" through their sensual capacities, they satisfy or further complicate my sense of desire as well as nostalgic and ontic qualities.

By observing "things" through there sensual capacities, past encounters with objects with similar features bring to bear the past, making those "things" attached with meanings vividly understood.

Kitson and McHugh (2015, 488; 489) argue that "it is precisely the amorphous and *sensual* qualities of nostalgia that make it a propulsive force in dwelling. . . . Whether an object, an idea, or a meteorological event, all materialities have agency and existence if they have the capacity to *affect*."

Furthermore, "things" engender aesthetics: aesthetics inherently have a pull and/or push factor that orients our body (or senses) toward particular "things" and people. Additionally, aesthetics—as intensities—force our attention to experience with them; they move us between levels of experience (i.e., preconscious, conscious, and post-conscious). To borrow from Sara Ahmed (2008, 51), "when things are orientated they are facing the right way: in other words, the objects around the body allow the body itself to be extended. When things are orientated, we are occupied and busy. The 'point' of this occupation might even make the face of the object recede from view. Occupation is hence not just about 'any body,' for an object tends toward some bodies more than others, depending on 'the tendencies' of bodies."

If we consider aesthetics to be the intensities between bodies/"things"/objects that orient us toward other bodies/"things"/objects, we are almost already oriented toward an understanding of the world-for-us and the world-for-Black-LGBTQ-people. This orientation is a process that happens alongside introspection. For example, my gaze and body are naturally oriented toward images of queer figures such as James Baldwin, Bayard Rustin, and Essex Hemphill because of the affective introspection that occurs from my gaze and orientation. The aesthetics engendered in the image are the force behind and beyond my orientation. As a result of this cognition, I come to understand the place-for-me, similar to the way Black LGBTQ people understand Black LGBTQ space for them.

Ultimately, in chapter 1, I suggest that Black queer placemaking is an act that resists the institutionalization and normalization of anti-Blackness, homophobia, economic deprivation, and spatial segregation. In chapter 2, I explore how Black queer people resist these same forces through world-making.

Chapter 2: Black Queer World-Making

Centered in field observations at Langston's, but also including interviews with former patrons of the Starlite and Warehouse clubs, chapter 2 focuses on Black queer world-making. I define Black queer world-making as a practice by Black queer people to establish territory where they exercise their agency and engage in practices that dominant society defames. I focus heavily on what Black queer people *do* in Langston's, including gesturing, speaking, naming, and "gettin' yo' life." According to queer performance theorist Juana María Rodríguez (2014, 6), gesturing "is a socially legible and highly codified form of kinetic communication, and . . . a cultural practice that is differentially manifested through particular forms of embodiment." Speaking, too, has implications beyond the mere content of the words. Speech acts may be used, for example, "to affirm, to command and to supplicate, to promise," and so on. In chapter 2, I suggest that Black queer vernacular (Richardson 2013)—"chile," "sis," "queen," among other terms—is used to create worlds that turn normative social codes on their heads to produce a new way of being and knowing. Naming is the act of labeling through language—in written *and* visual forms. For example, framed images of Black LGBTQ pioneers such as Langston Hughes that are affixed to each of the four walls in Langston's are a naming practice. The framed images mark Langston's as a historically attuned space.

Chapter 2 also introduces readers to the title concept of the book, "gettin' yo' life," which refers to the act of expressing meanings through the body, language, and interpersonal relationships. Grayson, one of the attendees of Langston's I interviewed, mentions the phrase while discussing how demographic concerns impact the underlying experience of a place. He states, "It's kind of up for debate, but I think it's important fundamentally for us to have a space for Black and gay men or bisexual men to, you know, congregate and 'Get yo' life.'" Here Grayson suggests a place or world in which to see people who look like you, converse, hook up, and spatially represent Black LGBTQ culture. Whether or not that space looks aesthetically pleasing or fitting in with the rest of the environment is secondary to "getting your life." The conditions under which you "get yo' life" are forged by care-work, performance, and kinship labor.

Chapter 3: Care-Work, Kinship Labor, and Performance

In the third chapter, I argue that another club, Happiness Lounge, is a community of care with a Black queer sense of place where Black LGBTQ people perform care-work and kinship labor and engage in performance that places queerness at the center. I provide examples of care-work, kinship labor, and performance unique to Happiness Lounge and discuss care-work at the lounge by focusing on the events that are organized there, such as a patron's solo vocal performance.

Care-work consists of the everyday and often taken-for-granted actions by which a person or people ensure the well-being of another person or group of people. In chapter 3, for example, I reflect on the Happiness Lounge bartender's suggestion that Montae, a patron, should come over for dinner. The bartender does not simply extend a frivolous dinner invitation. The bartender demonstrates a level of care-work that is rooted in a necessity to ensure well-being for Montae.

Marlon M. Bailey (2014) discusses kinship as a social connection to other people, and the actual work of making those connections, often through language, and their maintenance is kinship labor. As I discuss in chapter 3, the people inside of Happiness Lounge do kinship labor, creating connections with other people—in my case, an older man referred to me as "brotha." Using "brotha" is similar to calling someone "family," two terms that are used frequently in Black vernacular culture (Richardson 2013). Kinship labor is also represented through the recognition of people's birthdays using a public calendar, checking on the health of patrons who were recently in the hospital, and supporting people who are coming out to family.

Performance labor is the actual work or strategies that people do. It touches personal, political, and social spheres. José Muñoz (1999) relies on queer performances—which are inherently political—to conceive, forge, and execute survival strategies such as disidentification. Queer performances are also social in that they are honed and crafted in relation to other people, at times. Queer performances are personal to the extent that they are unique to a person's embodied histories and feelings. In chapter 3, I discuss Ballroom culture as a source of vital queer performance.

Methodology

My theoretical edifice, Black queer spatiality, and its epistemological expectations are informed by Black feminism (reflexivity and intersectionality), queer theory (sexuality as a vector of power), queer of color critiques (racial capitalism and desire), and worlding. The epistemological expectations in my investigation include combating misrepresentation and maximizing accountability. Black feminist epistemologies assume that there are multiple perspectives of knowledge (Arvin et al. 2013; Brown 1992). Queer of color critiques offer theories of racialized gender and sexuality as well as racialized flows of capital that socioeconomically deprive Black queer people (Ferguson 2004) that I can use to understand conditions of space- and placemaking (Bailey 2013; Manalansan 2003).

Furthermore, queer of color critiques oppose theories that are rooted in white supremacy and patriarchy—two hegemonic structures that regulate identities—that get built into the norms that dominant society claims as gospel (Baderoon 2011; A. Smith 2006; Foucault 1990; M. Alexander 2005). I discuss epistemologies and methodologies that help me understand the racialization of queer urban space. Black feminist epistemologies focus on differences among women and question the idea that there exists a "women's perspective" (Collins 2000). Therefore, Black feminism demands that I assume multiple truths exist because my interlocutors have varying relationships to hegemonic power structures. There are multiple relations to power that cannot be equated (Brown 1992; Crenshaw 1989; Hill Collins 2000; Bowleg [1971] 2012). To identify and analyze truths/knowledges about spatial marginalization, I must contend with reflexivity and intersectionality. Reflexivity and intersectionality are activist and postmodern modes of analysis that interrupt logics and practices of domination. According to Virginia Eubanks (2009, 117), "reflexivity, social location and intersectionality provide resources for undertaking feminist participatory research that is attuned to the dangers inherent in studying and speaking others' lives, and yet oriented towards developing a politics and a practice of alliance through collective political struggle."

Given how *Get Yo' Life: Black Queer Placemaking* centers Black queer people, my methodology takes up intersectionality to recognize that not only are race and gender co-constitutive (Crenshaw 1989; Bowleg [1971] 2012; Hill Collins 2000), but class and sexuality should be equally regarded as well. Bowleg ([1971] 2012, 1268) names the core tenants of intersectionality as follows: "(1) social identities are not independent and unidimensional but multiple and intersecting, (2) people from multiple historically oppressed marginalized groups are the focal or starting point, and (3) multiple social identities at the micro level (i.e., intersections of race, gender, and SES) intersect with macrolevel structural factors (i.e., poverty, racism, and sexism) to illustrate or produce disparate health outcomes." Brown (1992) demonstrates that I need to recognize not only differences (characterized by relations to power) but also the *relational* nature of those differences. So, intersectionality gives me a vocabulary to theorize the ways in which structural forces shape social identities and spatial formations.

Reflexivity forces me to center the body as a site of knowledge (England 1994; Moss 2002). Moss (2002) contends that feminist research practices in the social sciences require scholars to direct attention to the contexts of their research and reflect on spatial arrangements, attire, relationship-building, and the interplay of trust, friendship, and authority between researchers and participants. Thus, I take up reflexivity to break away from unequal power dynamics between myself and my interlocutors to build trust. Together, reflexivity and intersectionality hone my methodology such that it conceives methods that are participatory and transformative. In other words, reflexivity and intersectionality widen the possibility for achieving my epistemological expectations and, by extension, destabilize normalizing structures that continue to sociospatially marginalize my interlocutors. Considering that Black feminist epistemology has historically undertheorized desire, I rely on queer of color critiques (Somerville 2000; McGlotten 2012) to posit desire as a legitimate source of knowledge.

Queer theorist Chad Heap (2009) argues that queering an analysis positions sexuality within multifaceted constellations of power. However, queer theory fails to consider the various ways that sexuality is almost always racialized, which, in turn, informs reactions to and engagements with space, place, and citizenship—belonging. Manalansan (2003), for example, argues that "citizenship requires more than the assumption of rights and duties; it also requires the performance and contestation of the behavior, ideas, and images of the proper citizen." Queer of color critiques, then, are epistemological interventions that are poststructuralist. Poststructuralism challenges a notion of a pre-constituted sexual subject, understanding power as a production and a network and situating its theoretical energies toward the advancement of a critical approach that interrogates the politics of cisgender white heteronormativity.

Ferguson (2004, 3) contends that "queer of color critiques approach culture as one site that compels identifications with and antagonisms to the normative ideals promoted by the state and capital." So, queer of color critiques, such as Ferguson's (2004), understand the state to be a mechanism that exploits racial, sexual, and class minorities and justifies its actions as a social necessary for the reproduction of society through anti-Black policymaking. Ferguson (2004) explains the connection between heteronormativity as a social formation and capital, neoliberalism as well as racial capitalism.[1] Queer of color theories see the state and capital as two co-constitutive mechanisms that dominate my interlocutors in various ways. In addition, intersectionality has been refined by its current applications in queer of color critiques' theorizations of capital and its mode of critique known as historical materialism. According to Ferguson (2004, 11), capital is a site of perversions and contradictions; it is a "formation constituted by discourses of race, gender, and sexuality, discourses that implicate nonheteronormative formations like the

---

1. Racial capitalism is an economic system through which the built environment, ideas, and knowledge, as well as sign systems and feelings, are organized into different kinds of places to facilitate the extraction of surplus value (Ellison 2016, 326).

prostitute" who is pictured on the cover of his book. To be clear, commodity production erases subjectivity and agency. Ferguson (2004, 7) reminds us of Marx's words: "Commodification produces man as a mentally and physically dehumanized being, deforming agency and distorting subjectivity." Ferguson (2004) goes on to argue that as capital produces surplus populations, it provides the contexts out of which nonheteronormative racial formations emerge. Thus, the sex worker proves capital's defilement of man. She symbolizes dehumanization or feminization under capitalist modes of production. The point here is that intersectionality is shaped by perversions and contradictions that are characteristic of its social system—capitalism and its surrogate, the state. By perversions and contradictions, I am referring to the interdependence of capital and the state as it obliges normative prescriptions of race and gender and conceals and produces racial violence; however, capital without the state assembles labor without regard for normativity.

Black feminism, Black queer theory, and queer of color critiques are theoretical frameworks that support my methodology and epistemic expectations. Maximizing accountability and combating misrepresentation are expectations that respond to the implication that doing research with sociospatially marginalized people means that they are predetermined subjects devoid of epistemic privilege.

To maximize accountability to and combat misrepresentation of my epistemic community, I deploy critical ethnography to produce knowledge *with* my interlocutors. Critical ethnography, according to D. Soyini Madison (2012, 5), "is a method that begins with an ethical responsibility to address processes of unfairness or injustice within a particular lived domain." Therefore, critical ethnography has epistemic expectations that seek to raise awareness of injustice. For example, Madison (2012) mentions intersubjectivity while explaining that critical ethnography is a collaborative practice. Madison (2012) says:

> Striving toward an enlightened and involved citizenship also means that, although formerly the focus was on subjectivity relative to the Subjects, it must now move to intersubjectivity relative to the audience. Because performance asks the audience to 'travel' empathically to the world of the Subjects and to feel and know some of what they feel and know, two life worlds meet and the domain of the outsider and insider are simultaneously demarcated and fused. (478)

Critical ethnography challenges me to delve more deeply into the desires, and by extension, the social worlds of my interlocutors and engage the voices within the experience. Furthermore, critical ethnography is a surrogate of feminist epistemologies that necessitate intersectionality (Crenshaw 1989) and reflexivity (Eubanks 2009) in its constitution and execution. My approach to critical ethnography helps me investigate the extent to which language of space is language about politics, epistemologies, subjectivities, and desires. My approach helps me capture the conditions of and responses to spatial marginalization at scale.

My approach to critical ethnography considers intersectionality a theory and method that argues there are multiple perspectives (mine included); intersectionality helps me develop themes around spatial marginalization. Intersectionality is a theory and method insofar as it guides meanings for criticism. Madison (2012) argues that theory is a mode of interpretation; it is a method, yet it can be distinguished from method when a set of concrete actions grounded by a specific scene are required to complete a task. Bailey (2013, 2014), for example, uses a research methodology that is rooted in Black feminism[2] because he takes up intersectionality as a theory and method to expose differential power relations that characterize Black LGBTQ social life.

My approach to critical ethnography understands reflexivity as an ethical practice that is dialogic and transcends "written" culture to examine the body as a site of embodied knowing and sensations. Dwight Conquergood and E. Patrick Johnson (2013) postulate that the aim of dialogic performance is to bring self and other together so they may question and challenge each other. Considering this, my approach understands reflexivity as practice that cannot be devoid of the interplay between race and gender, as well as intersubjectivity. In other words, dialogue—a performance within critical ethnography—emphasizes the living communion of felt sensing, which, according to Madison (2012, 14), is an embodied interplay and engagement between human beings. At the same time, my approach relies on queer of color critiques to understand that sexuality and space are two vectors of power—alongside race, class, gender, and ability—that respond to spatial marginalization considering anti-Blackness and socioeconomic deprivation. I contend that there will be multiple responses that I must collect in the form of field notes, but I must write about my own experience and sensations that make Langston's what it is, and what it is not. Alison Bain and Catherine Nash (2006, 99) remind me that "the researching body cannot be understood as stable or fixed; rather it needs to be rendered explicitly visible [as] a contested site of knowledge production."

Sensation is a bodily happening that is an important dimension of spatiality that should be documented and analyzed so I can make a sound case that

---

2. By definition, Black feminisms are social justice projects that are dynamic, changing with the social conditions that block self-definition; they describe oppressive social organization.

Black spatiality is a praxis that aims to dismantle the colonization and white supremacy that affect and justify spatial marginalization. Critical ethnography is a tool that allows me to document and politicize my own sensation alongside my interlocutor's actions in the context of gender, class, scale, space, and place. Nadine Levy (2016) argues that fieldwork and emotions (what I consider a sensation, like nostalgia) pose methodological dilemmas. She goes on to say that working mindfully with emotions in the field provides researchers a richer understanding of the ideologies, emotion rules, and expectations tacitly operating in the site under investigation, which can in turn lead to crucial findings and fresh ways of seeing the research topic at hand. Similarly, I maintain that fieldwork and sensations are radical affects that support vectors of power (i.e., space and sexuality) to dismantle hegemonic power structures that condition the lives of my interlocutors. To further this point, Ruth Wilson Gilmore (2002, 15) argues that "the political geography of race consists of space, place, and location as shaped simultaneously by gender, class, and scale." Therefore, gender, class, and scale are categories of analysis—vectors of power—that substantiate the territoriality of power. Be that as it may, critical ethnography allows me to write my body in my research, noting my own sensation's experience relative to my interlocutor's and Langston's. It gives me the opportunity to investigate—through field notes—how sexuality operates to make Langston's what it is and is not. According to Foucault (1990, 49), "sexuality is a historical formation that involves bodies and pleasures; it is where intensity of pleasures converges and where persistency of power catch hold." Thereby, critical ethnography is a tool that produces multiple narratives as sites of ruptures in the territoriality of power.

Using worlding, the writing practice used to animate placemaking, Black queer spatiality aims to destabilize structures of power that create conditions that necessitate Black queer space—whether physical or cyber—as a means through which Black queer survival, joy, desire, and intimacy are predicated. Yet it is space that emplaces practices of encounter and space that carries inherent qualities of atmosphere, nostalgia, and sensations. Thus, Black queer spatiality attends to sites of encounter to further substantiate its theoretical edifice, while at the same time applying it as a method to identify and describe atmosphere of a particular place, nostalgia, and sensations that are unique to Black queer spaces and people.

Kitson and McHugh (2015, 490) say that nostalgia "is the sensory experience of desire for some*thing* that is unnamable and unreachable, momentarily present in fleeting fragments. Susan Stewart (1984) intones nostalgia as the 'desire for desire' that cannot be quelled." In other words, once the trace is realized by the body and the space it occupies no longer exists to experience desire through the body, then the body longs for this desire. Take for instance the framed images of Langston Hughes affixed to the walls of Club Langston, which are both affective and nostalgic as they initiate some*thing* that is presently fleeting or slipping away while being artifacts that are reminiscent of cultural, political, and personal meanings of the Harlem Renaissance era.

Additionally, sensations are felt responses to what is happening in a certain place and time. For example, sensations are physical reactions to happenings such as feeling warm in an overcrowded nightclub or the smell of Langston's when it is filled with people, coupled with mist from fog machines. All things considered, sensations have the capacity to affect nostalgia and atmosphere, simultaneously.

Fieldwork

Get Yo' Life centers the lived experience of Black queer people by focusing primarily on semiprivate, LGBTQ marked places such as Langston's and Happiness Lounge as well as public places in Brooklyn. My research field sites are marked Black LGBTQ social places across Brooklyn's built environment that allow me to explore the relationship between gentrification, Black queer placemaking practices, and ontological conditions of Black queer space. By marked places, I mean places that have signage and/or an object like a pride flag on the facade of a structure, both of which would lead the public to perceive the site as a queer site. This is similar to how some Black-owned and women-owned businesses affix stickers and posters that read "Black-Owned Business" or "Woman-Owned Business." My exploration requires qualitative methods, including archival research, semi-structured interviews, and ethnography, to provide nuanced descriptions of place and to explore how Black queer people understand sensation, atmosphere, and nostalgia in relation to Black queer marked places. From April 2018 to April 2020, I engaged in critical ethnographic fieldwork inside and outside of the Barclays Center (an arena), Langston's, and the Happiness Lounge, as well as in Fort Greene, Downtown Brooklyn, Crown Heights, and the neighborhoods where these places are located and Black LGBTQ public events were held. Critical ethnography, according to D. Soyini Madison (2012, 5), "is a research method that begins with an ethical responsibility to address processes of unfairness or injustice within a particular lived domain" or geographic location. These methods were deployed to complete my investigation in the context of political economy, displacement, and state-sanctioned surveillance and interpersonal violence against Black LGBTQ people. In addition, I completed several interviews with Black queer-identified men who have gone to Langston's and/ or Happiness Lounge, former nightclub owners, anti-gentrification activists, and architectural designers who have close knowledge of the Pacific Park development project, including the Barclays Center Arena. I completed archival research at the Interference Archive (Park Slope, Brooklyn)—an open-stacks archive collection that includes social movement artifacts such as queer protest invites and posters—and the Brooklyn Historical Society (Brooklyn Heights), a Brooklyn public library that is dedicated to neighborhood change and gentrification and queer history, to name two collections that are relevant to my investigation. At the Brooklyn Historical Society, I utilized the H. Dickson McKenna collection, the Robert Vadheim Brooklyn neighborhood renewal and development collection, Voices of Brooklyn oral histories, a Bedford Stuyvesant urban renewal area map, and Brooklyn-based newspapers. These collections were used to trace historical and contemporary instances of Black queer spatial and bodily displacement while theorizing how Black queer people utilize Black queer nightclubs and other Black queer cultural sites to produce affirming places and worlds with supportive systems.

In addition, I utilized Marxist geographic knowledges including Neil Smith (1984) and David Harvey (1973, 1982, 2011) to discuss flows of capital and its accumulation over time. My project explores what Black queer people do in space while capital takes hold of urban space through gentrification, and by extension, causes displacement of Black LGBTQ people and public culture. In Brooklyn, gentrification and displacement impact Black LGBTQ public culture; it is squeezed out of Black queer social places (nightclubs and bars) in Brooklyn's social landscape. I ask: What sociogeographic strategies do Black LGBTQ people craft to ensure a public community of care in Brooklyn, New York? What is a Black queer sense of place?

Following my interdisciplinary background research, I began fieldwork. My initial visits to Langston's and Happiness Lounge included neighborhood observations from 11 a.m. to 3 p.m. for three days each week, well before I conducted separate ethnographies inside the spaces. I took the subway from the apartment I shared with my aunt to Fort Greene to Crown Heights, Bedford-Stuyvesant, and Downtown Brooklyn to walk through the neighborhoods and photograph the Pacific Park development project, including the Barclays Center. I often sat on public park benches to observe pedestrian circulation, user meeting locations, and the construction and renovation of new and existing structures in and around the Pacific Park development project. My neighborhood field notes focused heavily on the demographics of neighborhoods such as Bedford-Stuyvesant and Crown Heights, soundscapes, and the atmosphere or mood of the area, as well as my own bodily sensations.

In summer 2018, I visited Club Langston for five consecutive weekends, arriving Fridays around 11:30 p.m. and staying until 1:30 a.m. Saturday morning. My ethnography of Langston's included observing the wall materials, lighting design, demographics, soundscapes, and objects on the walls and inside. In summer 2019, I visited Happiness Lounge for five Friday nights for two hours each visit. My ethnography of Happiness Lounge focused on what people *did* in the space, including their care-work, performance, and kinship labor. My ethnographic fieldwork was supported by ten semi-structured ethnographic interviews. These ethnographic interviews were spontaneous conversations with clubgoers. I conducted these interviews with bartenders, patrons, and a DJ to understand how Black queer people make sense (meaning) and index sense (sensations).

Spatial Theorizing and Black Queer Spatiality

Get Yo' Life: Black Queer Placemaking rests at the intersection of three bodies of knowledge to introduce Black queer spatiality: (1) critical race theory, (2) gender studies, and (3) theories of spatial justice. These three bodies of knowledge underscore the ways in which race, gender, and sexuality are inherently spatialized, and to that end I can begin to understand how Black queer identities are spatialized due to the ways in which systems of oppression work in tandem with political institutions to squeeze out Black queer public culture. In other words, nonqueer people and corporations make places that disallow Black queerness to exist in public and semiprivate spaces. In response, Black queer people engage in placemaking: the practice by which Black queer people organize to mark places that allow—even celebrate—Black queer public cultural space. These spaces allow users to further understand and forge their identities through being in community with other users of the spaces.

One such celebration of Black queer space is the Ballroom community. In a documentary about Ballroom culture and vogue performance (MIC 2016), Martez Smith, founder of Keeping Community Alive Network,[3] claims, "Voguing is very much like medicine for me. You hear that beat and you get that feeling . . . I'm telling you it runs through your body. I can feel it in my fingertips. It is an out-of-body experience. Like you get up there and that adrenaline starts going and you hear the beat and, like, SNAP! You take off!"

---

3. The Keeping Community Alive Network is an advocacy program that aims to organize Ballroom conferences, arrange medical support, and create courses that preserve the history of Ballroom (MIC 2016).

Here Martez suggests that voguing is a deeply personal queer performance. Voguing (see figures 0.1 and 0.2a) and Black LGBTQ public culture are political in that the dance form and values were born out of ostracization. Michael Roberson, an adjunct professor at the New School, suggests the culture is an "intervention around being ostracized, around being marginalized out of your community" (MIC 2016). Voguing is also social in Ballroom, considering the competitive aspect of a ball: people compete to snatch and slay trophies and earn "legendary" status—a coveted position that many Ballroom participants work toward. Figure 0.1 is an image of Martez Smith voguing at the Apocalypse Ball (hosted by OTA) in a black-and-white Power Ranger suit. During the show, Martez walked down the T-shaped catwalk and bent his knees to allow his body to go closer to the wall. He moved his arms from each side of his body as he moved closer to the judges. His hands twisted constantly to the beat of the music. He stared directly at the judges as he moved closer to them. Figure 0.2a also shows a ball participant engaged in queer performance, specifically voguing. The performer in the foreground lies on the floor with his chest raised in a high arch, his hips on the ground and his knees close together. His wrists are bent to accentuate his quick hand movements. His neck is tilted to look toward the ceiling of the Hedrick Martin Institute.

Another example of celebratory performance despite marginalization is OTA (Open to All), a weekly mini-ball that showcases the various intergenerational talents within the Ballroom community (see figures 0.2b, 0.2c, 0.2d, 0.2e, 0.2f, 0.2g). OTA was not a part of my formal fieldwork, but information about OTA came to me through my interviews, and I attended an event in 2023, which I discuss further in the conclusion. OTA occurs every Monday at the woman-owned nightclub 3 Dollar Bill, in Brooklyn. According to OTA's website (https://www.opentoallent.com), their sponsors and collaborators include Parkwood Entertainment (*Renaissance: A Beyoncé Film*), Times Square Arts (OTA in Times Square 2021), *Brooklyn News* (OTA: Brooklyn News Edition and Halftime Show), and Solomon R. Guggenheim Museum (Uptown Underground Ball). The spatial formation of OTA is precisely a consequence of the aggregate of Black queer cultural spatial marginalization by processes of anti-Blackness and the economic deprivation that shuttered and necessitates Black queer placemaking elsewhere in Brooklyn. The need to create new elsewheres continues, for as I will discuss shortly, in the years since I have documented them, both of my primary ethnographic sites—Langston's and Happiness Lounge—have closed.

FIGURE 0.1. Voguing at the Apocalypse Ball. Used with permission from Martez Smith.

FIGURE 0.2A. Voguing in front of a crowd. Photograph by the author.

FIGURE 0.2B. An OTA participant with a handheld fan.
Used with permission from Timothy Tobias.

FIGURE 0.2C. Three OTA participants. Used with permission from Timothy Tobias.

FIGURE 0.2D. A femme OTA participant. Used with permission from Timothy Tobias.

FIGURE 0.2E. An OTA participant sporting an open shirt.
Used with permission from Timothy Tobias.

FIGURE 0.2F. Costumed OTA participants. Used with permission from Timothy Tobias.

FIGURE 0.2G. More costumed OTA participants.
Used with permission from Timothy Tobias.

Race and Gender

In *Appropriating Blackness*, E. Patrick Johnson (2003) sparks conversation around authentic Blackness in the context of hegemonic masculinity and the historic occlusion of queer Blackness by way of Marlon Riggs's 1995 documentary *Black Is . . . Black Ain't*. Although Johnson's text is interested in interrogating, through ethnography, the ways in which performance allows for the authorization of Black authenticity that is predicated on challenging or succumbing to essentialist notions of gender, race, and sexuality, his text highlights the kinesthetic potential of queer Blackness. The ways in which queer Blackness has challenged hegemonic masculinity and notions of racialized gender is informed, in many ways, by the movement of the body through space (even when the movement is due to influx of corporations and the condo class).

From a Kantian perspective, space is a container that engulfs Black queer cultural artifacts such as flags and banners and the phenomena of Black queer cultural events, including resource tables outside of OTA. The production of space is predicated on power, knowledge, and geography. Black queer spatiality manifests using the meanings attached to place ("making sense"). The meanings attached to places such as OTA and 3 Dollar Bill include Black queer performances, desirability, queer identity formations, and Black queer exclusivity as a result of interpersonal and state-sanctioned violence. Its exclusion is understood through the marking of its space and the performances that occur within.

Queer Blackness produces places, conditions even, that are socially and culturally significant to what Judith Butler (2005) in *Undoing Gender* calls a "livable life." Anti-Blackness, transphobia, queerphobia, and femmephobia are not newly minted forms oppressions, but rather, to use a Freudian lens, these oppressions are material iterations of dominant society's nostalgia and amnesia—twin details of memory and heterotopias. These oppressions, which are rooted in colonization and white supremacy, are almost always spatialized. Besides, colonization was a tension over land and property—place. In "Letter on Humanism" (1946), Martin Heidegger contends that the prerequisite for humanity is to be placed.

Theories of Spatial Justice

The late Edward Soja (2010) leans into the spatial turn that foregrounds spatial thinking alongside sociological and historical thinking to raise new possibilities for discovering hidden insights, alternative theories, and revised modes of understanding cityspace. This is critical to the ways in which he thinks through social justice and I theorize about the democratization of cityspace. For Soja (2010, 19), space is not an empty void; it is critical to the flow of capital and is "always filled with politics, ideology, and other forces shaping our lives and challenging us to engage in struggles over geography." Soja (2010, 23) frames justice under the urban process of capitalism and contends that it "holds political meaning that transcends the defined categories of race, gender, class, nationality, sexual preference, and other forms of homogeneous and often exclusive group or community identity." There are four emergent geographical resolutions, according to Soja (2010), that inform spatial justice: unjust geographies (boundary making and the political organization of space), distributive justice (fair and equitable distribution of urban resources), distributional inequalities (individuals, firms, and institutions), and globalization of justice (meso-geographies).

Black queer spatiality, then, refers to a research method for examining what Black queer people do inside spaces, such as OTA, that are produced for and with other Black queer people who have been historically cast to the spatial and social fringes in Brooklyn's landscape. Black queer spatiality is established by identifying the ways in which bodily sensations *and* sense-making (understandings) manifest across a place, an interior. Black queer spatiality, moreover, is a humanistic social scientific method by which we recognize, interpret, and explain a Black queer sense of place as well as Black queer people's placemaking practices as sociospatial marginalization occurs.

In summer 2019, I conducted and analyzed semi-structured interviews with Black queer men who live/d in Brooklyn, including directors of Brooklyn-based nonprofit organizations focused on Black LGBTQ people, graduate students, health care workers, and City of New York housing coordinators. I developed and posted my request for interviews to academic listservs and social media platforms. Some people responded directly to my request via email, and other interviews were secured by my interlocutors making e-troductions to my project over email. Each interview lasted between one and two hours. Eight out of ten interviews were held in public places such as parks, restaurants, and sidewalks. In 2020 I pivoted from in-person interviews because of the COVID-19 pandemic, which grounded most flights (preventing my travel to New York City from Phoenix, Arizona) and closed most public places across the globe. As a result, two interviews were conducted virtually utilizing Zoom. Following my ten spontaneous ethnographic interviews and my formalized, semi-structured interviews, I identified the following themes: power, capital, public pressure, institutions, displacement, and place.

Furthermore, I engaged in archival research. (Photo)archiving was employed to visually document the current neighborhood conditions; interior conditions of the clubs, such as spatial configurations and floorplans; and Black queer people's actions and activities. Utilizing my ethnographic field notes, interviews, and archival data from the New York Department of Buildings and online news articles, I created a photo archive to understand the ownership history of the land beneath Club Langston and Happiness Lounge. The Department of Buildings supported my photography, and my photography supported the building data. The data from the Department of Buildings provided digital tax maps, summaries of neighborhood sales, building classification code data, and exchange-of-ownership information. This data clarified land/building ownership and provided neighborhood information, specifically Brooklyn's racial and economic data over time, zoning history, and records on elected officials. In addition to collecting data from the Department of Buildings, I conducted archival research at the Interference Archive in Park Slope (Brooklyn) to view protest material, including posters, communications, and flyers for Black Pride events, resource fairs, and letters discussing protests against homophobia. I used ArcGIS to provide visual representations of Brooklyn's Black population from 1990 to 2020. My photographs of Black queer performances, care communities such as Black Pride, and developments such as Pacific Park is an archive that visually clarifies the relationship between Black queer people and place, what I call Black queer spatiality.

Club Langston

Club Langston[4] was located at 1073 Atlantic Avenue and opened one month after 9/11 to provide a local outpost for Black LGBTQ people in Brooklyn, especially considering most people avoided Manhattan at the time. Calvin Clark, an older Black man, owned Langston's. Clark moved into Fort Greene (also called "the Black Chelsea" because it was an outpost for Black artists; Jordan 2019) in the 1980s. Langston's was located on the border of Crown Heights and Bedford Stuyvesant (Bed-Stuy). During the day, a black garage door covered the entrance door and there was no sign affixed to the facade of the two-story building to mark the space. A set of elevated train tracks were located to the left of Langston's and an auto parts store was located to the right. Once Langston's closed in 2019, Black LGBTQ people, particularly those who are over thirty years old, had one remaining neighborhood bar in Crown Heights, as the Black population had moved east over time. Figures 0.3, 0.4, and 0.5 show the change in Brooklyn's Black population from 1990 to 2020. The dark shaded areas represent a Black population of 1,000 people or more. Gray shaded areas refer to regions in Brooklyn that have a Black population of 500 people or more, while white shaded areas indicate a Black population of zero. As time progresses, the Black population in Crown Heights, Downtown, and Bed-Stuy decreases as Black people move further east.

---

4. Langston's was originally called Moor's Bar and Lounge.

FIGURE 0.3.
Brooklyn's Black
population, 1990.
Map completed by
author using ArcGIS.

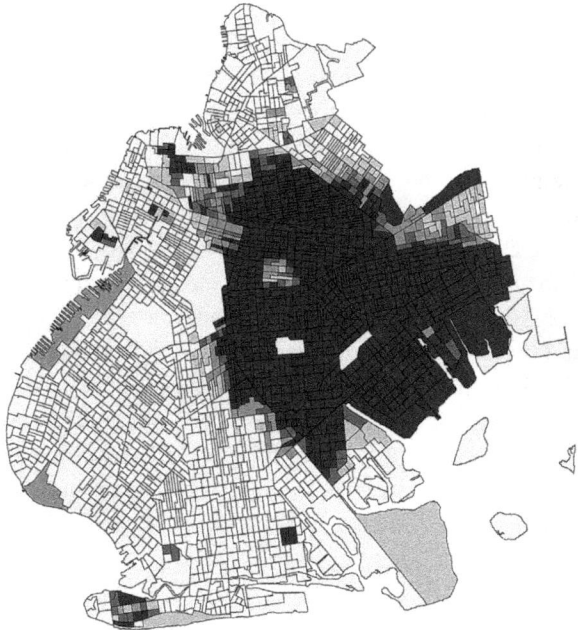

FIGURE 0.4. Brooklyn's
Black population, 2015.
Map completed by
author using ArcGIS.

FIGURE 0.5. Brooklyn's
Black population, 2020.
Map completed by
author using ArcGIS

On the weekends, soca, dancehall, and hip-hop music would fill the club and spill into the streets. "I lived in Flatbush and Bed-Stuy and there were a lot of Jamaicans and Haitians. I wasn't out of place when I lived there," Brian, one of my formal interviewees, said. Brian is a New York City transplant from Mobile, Alabama, who works in entertainment. After living in Brooklyn for several years, he moved to New Jersey with roommates. Brian's comments indicate that Langston's surrounding neighborhood influenced its weekend music playlist due to the concentration of Jamaicans and Haitians. Brian's comment also suggests that there is a high percentage of Black people in the Langston's surrounding neighborhood—Bed-Stuy.

As mentioned previously, Langston's closed in 2019 after Clark fell behind on the bills, as he had accumulated over $70,000 in back rent, taxes, and costs for city-mandated renovations. Prior to the shuttering of this black queer space, Calvin Clark wrote and performed a poem, "I AM A STAND," in protest. Presented on a white sign in front of Clark as he stood on a platform in front of Langston's, Clark's poem was both affective and nostalgic—nostalgic since it yearned for a vanishing space and affective through its cultural, political, and personal meanings. Its cultural meanings were found in words that express community-specific activities such as care-work. For example, Clark said, "I stand for us being loved and supported by family, friends, and community."

When he mentioned community support, he recognized that care-work is a fundamental practice in Black LGBTQ public culture. The poem's political meanings were found in the act of writing the poem and making the poem public to speak against the institutional policies that made it difficult for Clark to remain open. The personal meanings were found in Clark's statement, "My silence speaks loudly for those who live quietly in shame." This personal statement reflected Clark's individual performance of support, or care-work.

Inside Langston's now-empty building is a holiday wreath that hangs on the white eastern wall; pink, white, and burgundy holiday ornaments hang from the ceiling, and bells hang over the fire alarm at the main entrance. A mirror hangs on the back wall, and red ropes, speakers, chairs, and stools are stored in front the mirror toward the back of the bar. In addition, Clark's white poster is in the center of the space and leans against a tall, white column that stretches from the floor to the ceiling. The words of Clark's silent protest statement are written on the poster in black and red marker:

> I'm standing 10 days, not eating, not talking.
> A vow of silence, on Valentine's Day
> I will stand for 24 hours
> Please join me for a minute to bring awareness to Black LGBTQIA+ issues
> And reopen Langston's.

I further discuss Clark's silent protest later in this book (in chapter 2) as one example of how city land-use policies dislocate Black queer sensual geographies. In the case of Langston's, the state mandated expensive renovations that forced Clark to close the club, and this was coupled with the rising building rent costs due to the local gentrification exacerbated by the Pacific Park development project.

Spatial Marginalization

In Brooklyn, Black queer people are spatially marginalized through sociopolitical disenfranchisement and current gentrification in Brooklyn. Gentrification impacts Brooklyn by reconfiguring the landscape of race and class. Gentrification, as Neil Smith (1979, 547) notes, "is the process of converting working class neighborhoods into middle-class neighborhoods through the rehabilitation of a neighborhood's housing stock." In 2006 the Pacific Park project was approved. The Pacific Park project is located in downtown

FIGURE 0.6. The Pacific Park development project. Photograph by the author.

Brooklyn. Pacific Park[5] is an ongoing residential and commercial develop-ment project that includes luxury condominiums that rise seventeen stories and the Barclays Center. According to New York City–based journalist Jessica Dailey (2015), the condos at Pacific Park will hold 278 apartments, consisting of studios to four-bedroom units that will range from \$550,000 to \$5.5 million. Pacific Park—see figure 0.6—has negatively impacted Black LGBTQ public culture and necessitates the deliberate re-creation of Black queer space due to the geographical shift in Brooklyn's Black population and, at times, the extrac-tion of Black people from certain areas across Brooklyn.

Quality-of-Life Policy and Paradise Garage

In 1994 quality-of-life discourses were pronounced and their policy impli-cations burgeoned through New York City, stifling the ways in which Black LGBTQ people navigated the city and placing conditions on the ways in which they gathered in public. At the time, Rudy Giuliani[6] was the mayor of New York. Giuliani instituted a "stop and frisk" policy that, in reality, targeted Black people. The policy impacted the ways in which Black LGBTQ people expressed themselves in public and dictated the routes they took to navi-gate the city, the number of times they navigated the city, and the means by which they moved across the city. Effectively, Giuliani's "stop and frisk" policy created an atmosphere of police brutality and violence against Black people. Therefore, Black LGBTQ people's urban experiences—their quotidian reali-ties, social dynamics, and cultural expressions—were forged through nego-tiation. Additionally, under Giuliani's administration, Black LGBTQ people negotiated their approach to and circumstances within their urban environ-ments, which shifted with the flow of capital. In reality, Black LGBTQ people had to navigate a citywide policy that was laden with racism, classism, and sexism while forced to act in response to (in)direct and cultural displacement. For example, Black LGBTQ people's urban experience was not only shaped by "stop and frisk" but also gentrification, as white middle- and upper-class people flocked to the East Village and the Lower East Side (Manhattan) in

5. The Pacific Park project is adjacent to Brooklyn's Barclays Center. The project runs from Vanderbilt Avenue into Sixth Avenue.

6. In 2023, Giuliani was found liable for defaming Wandrea "Shaye" Moss and Ruby Free-man. Moss and Freeman were two Black women who were Georgia election workers. Giuliani falsely claimed that Moss and Freeman were tampering with votes during the 2020 election. Giuliani was also indicted in Georgia for his involvement in the insurrection on January 6, 2021 (Blake 2023).

droves, which prompted the Giuliani administration to prioritize community safety and morality in these areas particularly. Giuliani targeted people, places, and activities in the East Village and the Lower East Side because these neighborhoods were home to Black queer nighttime economies such as Paradise Garage.

In the late 1990s, the Giuliani administration formed a quality-of-life policing task force to squeeze out queer nighttime economies. The task force was responsible for ensuring nighttime economies were compliant with business rules. The primary business rule that the task force enforced was prohibiting dancing in an establishment that did not hold a cabaret license. New York City's Cabaret Law, passed and recognized in 1926, stated that "any room, place, or space in New York City in which patron dancing is permitted in connection with the restaurant business that sells food and/or beverages to the public requires a Cabaret license" (NYC Office of Nightlife, 2019).

The task force engaged in what William Bastone (1997) refers to as creative ticketing, the nonsensical ticketing of Black queer nighttime economies and its patrons, who were mostly Black queer and working-class people. Creative ticketing often followed new arrivals' noise complaints of queer nighttime economies to police. Paradise Garage, for example, closed due in part to its proximity to Greenwich Village and new residential developments in SoHo. Although Paradise Garage operated for ten years (1978–87) without complaint, its new neighbors were quick to denounce its existence and did not hesitate to call in noise complaints citing New York City's quality-of-life policy. Laam Hae (2011b) brings into focus the interconnectedness of anti-Black racism, socioeconomic deprivation, and homophobia:

> Paradise Garage is a prime example that demonstrates that even if the club is located in an appropriate place, it does not necessarily mean that the club could operate without problems, since the boundary of commercial, manufacturing, and residential land-uses was becoming more and more indistinct. In addition, the fact that the dominant patrons of the club were Black gays deterred favorable neighborhood relation to the club. Michael Brody, the owner of the club, claimed local residents "did not want a Black club in the neighborhood." (136)

Starting in the late 1990s, gentrification in the Lower East Side of Manhattan and Brooklyn intensified. To the local government, dance clubs created nuisance effects, such as publicized incidents of gun violence and drug trafficking. According to Hae (2011a, 570), "a wider range of nightlife businesses, such as bars, lounges, and restaurants, also became main targets of anti-night-life offensives by residential communities that suffered from these businesses' nuisance effects." Therefore, residents of the Lower East Side and Williams-burg, Brooklyn, for example, petitioned the State Liquor Authority to be cognizant of the number of liquor licenses it issued in neighborhoods that are overcrowded with nightlife businesses. This crackdown on alternative lifestyle businesses, starting in the late 1990s, disturbed Black LGBTQ public cultural formations, although Black queer people produced and maintained Black queer places elsewhere.

In early spring of 2024, I delivered a presentation in Brooklyn, New York. My presentation discussed the house music scene and Paradise Garage's significance to Brooklyn's Black queer community. After my thirty-minute presentation, an older Black man—aged sixty-four, I would soon learn—sauntered toward me. Anthony had short curly hair and wore large glasses that rested on the end of his nose. "Thank you for your presentation. I found it so interesting! It was nostalgic."

I replied, "Thank you so much. I appreciate you for sharing space with me and listening to some of the history of Paradise."

Anthony began to reach out for an empty chair to balance himself and slowly sat down. I sat next to him. "You know, I used to love Paradise!" he said. "I used to go there all the time because I love to dance, and nothing would compare to Paradise back then. Nothing at all. I would dance, spin all night."

I asked, "Oh, so Paradise was your go-to-spot?" Anthony replied,

Oh yeah. You know I would go, and I would dance all night and morning. DJ Frankie would have up in Paradise in a whole different world. You see DJ Frankie was the star at Paradise and around the world. He taught voguing around the world. Even Korea! I never would have thought our community would have so much popularity around the world. You know Frankie came to here to this school and taught a voguing class and the students really enjoyed it.

I said, "Frankie is truly a legend. Would you leave when the sun was coming up?"

Anthony smiled and said, "Until the sun was coming up? I wouldn't leave until 12 p.m. The sun was already up. Very much up! After I would leave Paradise, you know where I would go?"

"Where? I'm curious," I replied. With excitement and a head spin and a clap, Anthony said,

I would go to the Pink Tea Cup! You see the Pink Tea Cup is a after-Paradise eating spot. You know all that dancing, everybody would leave Paradise and go right over to the Pink Tea Cup. Most of the people you danced with in Paradise were at the Pink Tea Cup. You see the waiters would wear pink skirts and pink shirts. It was like a diner type of feel, and everyone would swallow down their pancakes and eggs. It was truly the after-spot.

Considering Anthony's reflection on Paradise Garage, it became clear to me that Paradise was a magnet, a refuge, for Black queer people to dance well into the next afternoon. However, while Anthony was sitting next to me, I wanted to know more Black queer sites that were nostalgic for him. I sat at the edge of my seat and asked Anthony, "I know you like to dance all night, so what are some other places you would go to besides Paradise?" He responded with a large smile,

I would go to the Loft, the Tunnel, and Nell's. These were all good places to go to and spin. The Loft was a decent place to go. The music was good, but I would go there as much as I would go to Paradise. You see the funny thing about the Loft was that they would charge $4.99 to get inside the club. At the entrance, before you got inside there was a large bowl full of pennies. The idea was that people would give the doorman a five-dollar bill and you would take a penny. It was full of pennies because it was a gimmick. It was free to get in, but it was a funny gimmick. Then there was the Ritz, which had a gay night. You know how that goes. Some places had gay nights that still happens today, you know. The Ritz looked like an older church in the village. It was real popular. Even the legend Tina Turner performed there. I wouldn't go too much because it was not like an exclusively Black LGBT place and the *bridgers* would come.

I asked with confusion, "What is a 'bridger'?" Then Anthony whispered, "A bridger is a white person from outside the community who would travel from Jersey to come to the Ritz's gay night." He pursed his lips, rolled his eyes, and burst into laughter.

Although he did not have to say it, I read his facial expressions as a means to say that not only was the Ritz not an exclusively Black LGBTQ place, but it felt like a tourist attraction for people outside of the Black LGBTQ community who could visit for a short period of time to experience the culture and then retreat back to Jersey to carry on with their lives. I thanked Anthony for sharing his time with me as he stood up and reached for his coffee cup. He sauntered out of the room.

Event Permit: Denied!

In the same year that the city approved the Pacific Park development project, People of Color in Crisis (POCC) was denied an event permit for Pride in the City at Commodore Barry Park, based on actions cited from 2005. POCC was one of the premier agencies in New York City and throughout the United States that served people of color infected and affected by HIV. POCC's level of activism was also reflected in their work in organizing events such as Pride in the City in Brooklyn and the creation of the Black Gay Research Group (BGRG). The Parks Department stated that POCC violated park policy in the following ways: (1) There were three times the maximum number of attendees allowed at Commodore Barry Park; (2) trash was not picked up at the end of the event; and (3) the Pride in the City event—a community of care, a Black queer space that affirms Black LGBTQ people—did not end at the required 9 p.m. curfew (Schindler, 2006). As a result, POCC cancelled Pride in the City in 2006.

Theory

Black queer spatiality is a humanistic-materialist mode of spatial inquiry and spatial activity that both explains and demonstrates a Black queer sense of place. According to humanist Edward Relph (1976), a sense of place requires a deep-rooted bond between people and place (cited in Hubbard et al. 2005, 42–43). Courtney Campbell writes, "Edward Relph . . . urges scholars to seek a more human-centred and empathetic understanding of 'the lived experience of place'" (2018, e26). I argue that space is a social construction constantly in transformation and spatiality is the practice of systematizing bounded sensation, identity, and meanings. Black spatiality, then, refers to the inquiry and spatial activity with particular focus on sensation, identity, and meanings through space, which, therefore, constructs place. Black queer spatiality refers to the dynamic between people and place.

A Black queer sense of place yields a deeper understanding of spatial production by Black queer people. In addition, a Black queer sense of place uncovers how Black queer people relate to the marked space—or bounded place—around them, how they make it their own (if only for a second!), and how they relate the bounded place to other places. Black queer spatiality is influenced by postmodern thought; it substantiates the postmodern notion that space is complex and socially constructed. As a method, Black queer spatiality indexes sensation, atmosphere, and nostalgia to bring to bear sensory data in and across an identified space. Black queer spatiality is also a spatial happening—a spatial typology that is constituted by Black queer people. Yet it is important to understand the intellectual context out of which Black queer spatiality emerges by first discussing Western conceptions of "space."

Western thought conceives of space as something that envelopes or encases social relations. However, Cavanagh (2010) challenges dominant articulations of public space by discussing the bathroom as a site where gender and sexuality are destabilized. She theorizes how and why the public bathroom is a space for gender-based hostility, anxiety, fear, and desire; the bathroom is a site of homoerotic desire in addition to social relations. In her theorization, "space is the mechanism by which we negotiate gender identity and social difference" (Cavanagh 2010, 12). Heidi J. Nast and Steve Pile (1998) argue that space is where the body is territorialized and deterritorialized. What this means is that space is where defense mechanisms, internalized authorities, intense feelings, and power and meaning converge (Cavanagh 2010, 11). Considering this, space is an environment also produced by Black queer people through spatial performance of race and gender, for example.

McKittrick and Woods (2007) contend that private and public spaces interact with one another, which calls into question spatiotemporal processes that undergird spatial articulations of race and gender. McGlotten et al. (2009, 226) raise a critical question that I explore in this book: What are the possibilities and probabilities of theorizing Black gender and sexuality in place-specific terms?

Furthermore, the influence of the postmodern turn of the 1990s brought into focus the ways in which Western conceptions of space—including space, place, and scale—have been epistemically narrow. The epistemic limitations provoked methodological and spatial debates that aim for deeper understandings of Western conceptions of space. In the 1970s, human geography emphasized two trajectories to spatial inquiry: humanism and Marxism. Humanistic approaches to spatial inquiry assume that different locations engender different senses of place. Furthermore, humanistic accounts of spatial inquiry focus primarily on lived-in space. Thereby, humanistic accounts contend that space is created through fields of care; conversely, place is saturated with meaning. Marxist approaches, however, assume that space is socially produced and consumed, and by extension, this approach focuses on domination and resistance relative to various spaces (P. Hubbard et. al. 2005).

In the 1990s, human geography took a postmodern turn. The postmodern turn expanded human geography's analytical frame such that the study of geography and social justice are intentionally linked. The analytical frame, moreover, focused on pluralities, binaries, positionalities, and deconstruction.

Therefore, human geography's postmodern turn destabilized notions of a universal definition for space as well as place. Instead, the postmodern emphasized space as a social construct. As a social construct, space is almost always transforming (P. Hubbard et al. 2005).

At the start of the 2000s, the spatial turn unabashedly linked social change to space; particularly, the spatial turn influenced spatial thinking that demonstrated the interconnectedness of social change and space. Therefore, social change is achieved through spatial means. Martina Löw (2013) discusses that social change cannot be achieved and explained without the spatial dimension of social life. Although some scholars have limited their approach to the spatial turn by focusing on methodological questions, the spatial turn additionally seeks to understand how spatial meaning is constructed and how space is represented. Yet across human scale, the spatial turn presents itself as a venture that aims to acquire a deeper understanding of geographic concepts and their inherent processes. This way space is understood as an approach to history, an object of analysis, and a methodology to comprehend further a distinct object of study (Campbell 2018).

In conjunction with postmodernism and Black queer spatiality, the spatial turn should further expand its methodological underpinnings. Western conceptions of space privilege physical spatial manifestations of social, cultural, economic, and political processes that provoke human behaviors in and across space. Cities such as New York have been conceived and perceived as the setting for social, cultural, economic, and political processes. Such processes are the objects of analysis under Western conceptions of space; they are fundamentally points of departure. Cities—built environments—are recognized as consequences of human behaviors at the interpersonal, institutional, and structural levels. Western conceptions of space—such as landscape (or built environment)—attend to the processes in and across built environments by constituting corrective solutions to human behaviors through social justice and spatial linkages.

Spaces are more than settings for human activity; these settings are more than where race, gender, class, and sexuality are realized. Spaces are co-constituted by sensory data including sensation, spatial atmosphere, and nostalgia. For example, sensory data can bring into focus environmental problems. Jennifer Kitson and Jonathan Bratt (2016) discuss cities[7] as a set of spatial processes that are implemented by people. In turn, people create environmental problems that shape their behavior. Western conceptions of space emerge

---

7. Kitson and Bratt (2016, 367) say that "cities are imaginations that are more than just setting for human activity; they are also constitutive of activity through the production of a 'sensory fabric' that envelops and impinges upon their inhabitants."

from those pivot points. By pivot points, I mean the points in time and space when people shift their behaviors based on consensus about an environmental problem.

Feminist geographers, such as Katherine McKittrick (2006) and Clyde Woods (McKittrick and Woods 2007), disturb theories of space. Feminist geographers' theorizations of space contend that private and public spaces interact with one another, which calls into question spatiotemporal processes[8] that bring into focus race and gender. McGlotten et al. (2009, 226) raise a critical question about the possibilities and probabilities of theorizing Black gender and sexuality in place-specific terms.[9] Black queer spatiality is a method and a theory to explain a Black queer sense of place. Black queer spatiality maps history to experience, attending to the sensorial and multiple dimensions of space and spatial articulations. Spatial articulations refer to the space sensed or understood by Black queer people, who have a particularly unique relationship to space. What this means is that a space includes spatial markers and signifiers that are recognized by Black and Black queer people.

Western conceptions of space and place provide a basic geographic framework that does not adequately incorporate an analysis of race, class, gender, and sexuality. It is as if geographic thought does a matrix backbend of sorts to avoid intersectionality (Crenshaw 1989) to reproduce theories that solely rest on capital. Space, for Henri Lefebvre (1991), is a commodity and a contradiction. It is where the state and its bureaucratic and political apparatuses converge. J. B. Jackson (1995, 24) defines space as a "whole community." He also says that the power of space is great, and it is always active for creation and destruction. Place, according to Tim Cresswell and Gareth Hoskins (2008, 393), has been conceived in various ways, but dominant notions have defined place as a "location, as a material setting for social relations, as a field of care and center of meanings, and as a coming together of disparate practices and flows." Therefore, Western conceptions and theorizations of space do not recognize the historical and current realities of Black people, let alone Black LGBTQ people. As a result, Black LGBTQ people produce their own spaces and places that uplift and legitimize their personhood.

Moreover, race, gender, and sexuality exist in space. As social constructions, they have a set of histories that have been written about, but the ways in which these histories or constructions have an inherent sensational quality lacks critical engagement. For example, Shaka McGlotten (2014) discusses queer performances, particularly cruising, in public spaces in Austin, Texas,

---

8. Spatiotemporal processes are those instances where space and time converge.
9. Place-specific terms include the geographic contexts of a situation, idea, or otherwise.

as well as online in chat rooms to discuss worlding. His discussion includes a particular focus on affective qualities that are inherent in physical public spaces and cyberspaces. His psychic geography calls into focus the relationship between space, sex, and feelings involved with worlding—a concept and method. Lauren Berlant (2009) defines worlding as a "concept in progress" and a method of describing that animates experiences rather than flattens them. Therefore, he argues that the way queer desire and cruising are performed in space should suspend the notion that race, for example, is ontological. McGlotten (2014) worlds an experience of a queer person of color in the private life of public queer spaces in Austin, Texas, who remembers an intimate encounter that was marked by racial exclusion.

Considering this lived experience, space, then, is a vector of power insofar as it is a sociospatial formation by which race, gender, and sexual minorities understand difference, affect, and desire. Also, space is a vector of power that emplaces spatial articulations of race, gender, and sexuality. This experience also calls into focus historical and current processes that create conditions for racial exclusion; the experience makes it clear that space is important for Black queer people's cultural expression across urban and rural areas, considering the way that McGlotten (2014) recounts a cyberspatial experience. The experience includes anti-Black racism conditions and spatial articulations, and I argue that a more comprehensive theory and method to understand the extent to which they are unique is required. Therefore, Black queer spatiality expands the epistemic and ontological dimensions of spatial articulations. Black queer spatiality theorizes spatial articulations by identifying historical processes of oppression produced by structures of power and felt by Black queer people.

CHAPTER 1

Waking Up in Aunt Jeanette's Place

It is a Saturday in late June 2019, and the Frigidaire alarm has awoken me at 9:30 a.m. Every morning, I wake up to the rattling sound of the window air-conditioner unit inside my aunt Jeanette's living room window. The small white air-conditioner unit is, in fact, my alarm clock for the duration of my stay with my aunt. "Frigidaire" is printed in gray on the left side of the air con-ditioner. Below "Frigidaire" are two white knob controls vertically situated: the top knob controls the speed while the bottom knob controls the temperature. The settings are "low," "high," "warm," and "cold," and my aunt Jeanette turns the unit on cold and high every morning.

Long beige sheer drapes fall from the top of the living room window against each side of the air-conditioner unit. The white, plastic window blinds are raised to top of the window, allowing the sunlight to shine effortlessly into the living room through the west-facing window. My body is stretched across the firm, tan sofa bed situated directly in front of the living room window AC unit.

After lying awake for five minutes, I hear the morning news coming from my aunt's bedroom, which is adjacent to the living room. My aunt religiously watches MSNBC every morning. Ten minutes later, there is a commercial break introducing prescription medications, new vehicles, and then silence because my aunt mutes the television during most commercials. A few sec-onds later, Aunt Jeanette emerges from her bedroom—where my great-aunt

Nettie Young's quilt hangs on her north wall—wearing a purple blouse, dark denim pants, and black platform sandals. "Good mornin'!" she says, walking to the kitchen. I say, "Mornin'." As she walks to the kitchen, I ask, "What's happening in the world?" This is my way of asking her about the news segments. To which she responds, "Everything . . . just everything is happening in the world." She pulls a can of instant coffee from the top cabinet and sets the orange can on top of the beige counter. After that, she fills her silver water kettle and places it on the stove. "Do you have any plans for today?" she asks me. "Yes, I'm going to over to Bed-Stuy. Spike Lee is hosting a block party on Do the Right Thing Way for the thirtieth anniversary of *Do the Right Thing*."

The Do the Right Thing block party is an example of Black public culture. The block party also makes place through naming a street after *Do the Right Thing*, Spike Lee's 1989 film exploring racial tensions in Bedford Stuyvesant over the course of one summer day. The film marked the beginning of a cultural movement and remains iconic. In addition to the film depicting Black consciousness, the film showcased examples of fighting systemic racism in the New York City context.

In the introduction, I discussed the historical geographies of Black queer spaces such as Paradise Garage. I discussed the ways in which anti-Black and anti-queer legislation undermined the possibilities of Black queer placemaking in Brooklyn from the 1960s to 2006. Also, I discussed how the Pacific Park mixed-use development project squeezed Black queer public culture out of Downtown Brooklyn's landscape and displaced working-class Black queer people. This chapter is about Black queer spatiality. First, I explore the ways in which Blackness and queerness come together to inform my spatial experience. Second, I recount how Black queer spatiality manifests under specific spatial and temporal conditions in my aunt's apartment. Third, I explore how Blackness manifests at a block party and investigate why and to what degree Black queer people are de/centered in a heteronormative space—that is, a space that is overwhelmingly populated by people who conform to a level of normativity that is predicated on opposite-sex relationships and acceptable gender performances, such as men nodding their heads to the music playing across the speakers and rocking side to side, and at the same time, women dancing in front of men, twerking with their hands in the air, and screaming when their favorite song plays. In this chapter, I discuss how Black queer people reject heteronormativity and engage in gender performances that oppose the aforementioned widely accepted gender performances in public.

Black queer people engage in placemaking through acts of naming, distinctive activities, and imaginings associated with a particular place. Acts of naming include public events that commemorate cultural movements such that mainstream society is aware of a particular site that is characterized by a set of human activities at a particular point in space-time. Moreover, acts of naming include conscious acts of affixing physical signifiers and meanings associated with distinct histories and lived experiences to a particular bounded place. In addition, distinctive activities include various performances that affirm Blackness and queerness in space, such as intimate dance and spatial reconfigurations, which thereby destabilize spatial articulations of gender-based hostility and anxiety. Black queer people, in addition, rely on gender, race, and class-based imaginings to constitute place in a way that aligns with their desirability, which, by extension, upsets the heteronormative attunements of dominant spaces and bounded places. I refer to dominant spaces as the spaces of public, everyday life; these spaces are where heteronormativity is palpable and regularly destabilized by sexual and gender minorities. By bounded places, I mean places that have an actual or iterative boundary or marking that distinguishes them from elsewhere. I demonstrate that Black queer people's comprehensive activities form Black queer spatiality. While this chapter focuses on what Black queer people do in public space, I argue these main points: Black queer people make interventions in public space to resist the erasure of Black queer public culture by structural powers, which is fundamentally a Black queer performance rooted in resistance; Black queer public culture includes materialized nostalgia; and sensations make clear the distinct dimensions of Black queer public culture.

Buggin' Out: I Want Some Brothas on the Wall of Fame

In 1999, *Do the Right Thing* was added to the National Film Registry. In 2015, the New York City Council approved the renaming of a one-block stretch of Stuyvesant Avenue (between Quincy Avenue and Lexington Avenue) as part of Bill No. 849-2015[1] (see figures 1.1 and 1.2). Do the Right Thing Way was the only renaming in 2015 that paid tribute to both an artistic production and a cultural movement to resist systemic racism.

Back at my aunt's house, Aunt Jeanette nods her head to acknowledge my plans to attend the block party. She then smiles and says, "I'm going to see my grandbaby today in Queens. I may be there all day because Sekou [her son]

---

1. The legislative text was written by the Speaker (Council Member Mark-Viverito) and Council Members Arroyo, Barron, Cabrera, Constantinides, Cornegy, Crowley, Cumbo, Dickens, Gibson, Johnson, King, Koo, Levin, Levine, Maisel, Matteo, Menchaca, Mendez, Miller, Reynoso, Richards, Rodriguez, Rose, Treyger, Vacca, Vallone, Van Bramer, Williams, Deutsch, and Kallos.

File #: Int 0849-2015, Version: *

Preconsidered Int. No. 849

By The Speaker (Council Member Mark-Viverito) and Council Members Arroyo, Barron, Cabrera, Constantinides, Corney, Crowley, Cumbo, Dickens, Gibson, Johnson, King, Koo, Levin, Levine, Maisel, Matteo, Menchaca, Mendez, Miller, Reynoso, Richards, Rodriguez, Rose, Treyger, Vacca, Vallone, Van Bramer, Williams, Deutsch and Kallos

A Local Law in relation to the naming of 51 thoroughfares and public places, Henry "Red" Allen Way, Borough of the Bronx, Tanaya R. Copeland Avenue, Borough of Brooklyn, Gregorio Luperón Way, Borough of the Bronx, Dennis Syntilas Way, Borough of Queens, Do The Right Thing Way, Borough of Brooklyn, Detective Clarence M. Surgeon Way, Borough of Brooklyn, Bishop Joseph M. Sullivan Way, Borough of Queens, Frank Kowalinski Way, Borough of Queens, Gus Vlahavas Place, Borough of Brooklyn, Leonard Harper Way, Borough of Manhattan, P.O. Ronald G. Becker, Jr. Way, Borough of the Bronx, Maxine Sullivan Way, Borough of the Bronx, Larry Selman Way, Borough of Manhattan, Sgt. Charles H. Cochrane Way, Borough of Manhattan, Carmen Rosa Way, Borough of the Bronx, Allison Hope Liao Way, Borough of Queens, Briana Ojeda Way, Borough of Brooklyn, Dorothy Skinner Way, Borough of Manhattan, Robert Lowery Way, Borough of Manhattan, Firefighter John P. Sullivan Way, Borough of Manhattan, Peter W. Piccininni Way, Borough of Brooklyn, Captain James McDonnell Way, Borough of Manhattan, William Soto Way, Borough of Manhattan, Dr. Meryl Efron Way, Borough of Staten Island, Mrs. Rosemary Way, Borough of Staten Island, Officer Thomas Choi Avenue, Borough of Staten Island, Assistant Principal Linda A. Romano Place, Borough of Brooklyn, Rabbi Sidney Kleiman Way, Borough of Manhattan, Detective 1st Grade Brian Moore Way, Borough of Queens, Vincent Abate Way, Borough of Brooklyn, Mitchell-Lama Way, Borough of Brooklyn, Detective Dennis Guerra Way, Borough of Queens, Sheila Pecoraro Way, Borough of Queens, James English Way, Borough of Queens, Mary's Way, Borough of Queens, Matty Alou Way, Borough of Manhattan, Albert Blumburg Way, Borough of Manhattan, Bruce Reynolds Way, Borough of Manhattan, EMT Luis De Pena Jr. Square, Borough of Manhattan, Elizabeth Egbert Way, Borough of Staten Island, Dominick (Dom) Lambert Way, Borough of Staten Island, Art Hall Way, Borough of Staten Island, Wayne "Chops" Derrick Way, Borough of Staten Island, Louis Powsner Way, Borough of Brooklyn, Father Connie Mobley Boulevard, Borough of Brooklyn, Seth Kushner Way, Borough of Brooklyn, Bill Twomey Place, Borough of the Bronx, Ptl. Phillip Cardillo Way, Borough of Queens, Matinecock Way, Borough of Queens, Marjorie Sewell Cautley Way, Borough of Queens and Catherine McAuley High School Way, Borough of Brooklyn

Be it enacted by the Council as follows:

Section 1. The following street name, in the Borough of the Bronx, is hereby designated as hereafter indicated.

New Name	Present Name	Limits
Henry "Red" Allen Way	Prospect Avenue	Between Freeman Street and East 169th Street

FIGURE 1.1. Text of Bill No. 849, page 1. Retrieved from https://www.nyc.gov.

File #: Int 0849-2015, **Version:** *

§2. The following intersection name, in the Borough of Brooklyn, is hereby designated as hereafter indicated.

New NamePresent NameLimits		
Tanaya R. Copeland Avenue	None	At the north side of Stanley Avenue and Schenck Avenue

§3. The following intersection name, in the Borough of the Bronx, is hereby designated as hereafter indicated.

New NamePresent NameLimits		
Gregorio Luperón Way	None	At the southern corner of Burnside Avenue

§4. The following street name, in the Borough of Queens, is hereby designated as hereafter indicated.

New NamePresent NameLimits		
Dennis Syntilas Way	30th Avenue	Between 29th Street and 30th Street

§5. The following street name, in the Borough of Brooklyn, is hereby designated as hereafter indicated.

New NamePresent NameLimits		
Do The Right Thing Way	Stuyvesant Avenue	Between Quincy Avenue and Lexington Avenue

§6. The following street name, in the Borough of Brooklyn, is hereby designated as hereafter indicated.

New NamePresent NameLimits		
Detective Clarence M. Surgeon Way	Rochester Avenue	Between Atlantic Avenue and Herkimer Street

§7. The following street name, in the Borough of Queens, is hereby designated as hereafter indicated.

New NamePresent NameLimits		

The New York City Council — Page 2 of 11 — Printed on 4/14/2022

powered by Legistar™

FIGURE 1.2. Text of Bill No. 849, page 2. Retrieved from https://www.nyc.gov.

must work in the afternoon." Sekou is a dark-skinned Black man in his late thirties who performs as a comedian across the city. His family lives in Long Island City, which is on the west side of Queens, New York. After five minutes of listening to my aunt's afternoon plans with "her baby," as she calls her, the silver tea kettle starts whistling. "C'mon, get some coffee. You can't start the day without a cup," she yells to me. I slowly rise up and notice markers of Blackness throughout the apartment.

Black cultural objects in my aunt's apartment include the stack of *Essence* magazines, a photo of Michelle Obama on a small table, and a copy of *The Quilts of Gee's Bend* (Rubin 2017). *Gee's Bend* is a book that showcases the history and culture of Black feminists in Gee's Bend, Alabama,[2] including my great aunt, Nettie Young. My aunt Nettie's quilt *Stacked Bricks* features multicolored rectangles in three columns that resemble bricks and a horned, yellow animal throughout the quilt. Brandi Thompson Summers (2019) reminds us that

> Blackness connotes symbolisms and significations of Black subjectivity and identification. Furthermore, Blackness has salience across different time periods and geographies. The evolution of Blackness as an engine of profit represents one of the most remarkable transformations of the modern era. An economy of symbols built on anti-Black caricature cultivated the world of golliwogs, Aunt Jemima Pancake Flour [now Pearl Milling Company], and blackface minstrelsy. Since the mid-twentieth century, however, the incorporation and appropriation of Black self-fashioning, blackness-as-taste, blackness-as-style, blackness-as-struggle, and blackness-as-nostalgia into mainstream markets have created a new medium of racial representation, consumption, and commercial growth, which conceal the violence of dispossession and highlight the illusion of inclusion within the culture of modern capital. (3)

Summers's (2019) statement recognizes that Blackness is often removed from Black identity and experience; Blackness is aestheticized for white consumption at the neighborhood scale. However, the Black-centric objects in my aunt's apartment (a private space) are not for aesthetics. Rather, these objects are political insofar as they represent a history of Black resistance and heritage and catalyze the production of a private Black space by Black people. Yet as a

2. Gee's Bend, Alabama, is a small, rural town with a population of approximately seven hundred who are mostly descendants of slaves. For generations, the residents worked the fields belonging to the local Pettway plantation and created quilts dating back to the 1920s (https://www.soulsgrowndeep.org/publication/gees-bend-architecture-quilt).

gender and sexual minority who is tethered to my aunt's apartment—a site of rich Blackness—I seek to understand how Blackness, gender, and sexuality are spatiality articulated by Black queer people and how the spatial articulation is sensed in public, a contested space.

Blackness is a lived experience that has historically been vilified; at the same time, it has been the real estate upon which cultural extraction and appropriation occurs for the advancement of US popular culture. The legacy of chattel slavery in the US has had reverberating consequences for Black people across several generations from social, political, and economic discrimination; an intense reckoning with police (state) brutality; uneven development that impacts health and wellness outcomes for Black women and children; and the misrepresentation of Black people in the media globally. That said, because of my own Black queer body, though surrounded by Blackness—nostalgic and contemporary—I feel that I am pressured to conform to my aunt's ontological Blackness (heteronormativity) because I want to ensure that my Black queerness is protected inside of the apartment's walls. I do not want to end up having an intense argument about my sexuality, a situation I have seen many friends and associates navigate. The truth is, this is an assumption on my part, because I never sat down to talk to my aunt about my sexuality because I am simply who I am. Yet, this is an every day and night occurrence for most Black queer people navigating a world that does not want them to exist. My aunt looks at me as I stare at my cup. "What's wrong?" she asks. "Nothing," I say with a smile.

I open the cabinet for a coffee mug and notice an "Obama" magnet on the side of the refrigerator and a framed photograph of Michelle and Barack Obama leaning against the wall. I pull a medium-sized, blue-colored coffee mug out of the cabinet, and my aunt pours the instant coffee into the blue mug. As she pours the coffee, its deep chocolate aroma dances in and across my nose and eventually fills the air of the apartment.

"I want you to see what I got my baby!"

I stand in the middle of the kitchen sipping the hot, aromatic dark-roasted instant coffee. My aunt walks to a hall closet to the right of the bathroom. She pulls out a large brown-and-white box. "Activity Gym" is printed in black letters across the top and side of the box. "I can put it together at Sekou's later this week and leave it there. My baby is getting all my attention while I'm there. What you think about it?"

"It's nice . . . I think she will love it," I reply.

"Yeah, I think she will love it. It has pinks and purples. She will love it! She loves those colors."

I take a sip of my coffee.

"I should be going, then. I want to get there way before Sekou leaves for work." She grabs her black leather purse and throws it across her shoulder before walking out of the apartment. I lean against the refrigerator gazing at the "Obama" magnet on the side of the refrigerator.

Black Queer Placemaking

Similar to the means by which Blackness shows up in semiprivate and public spaces, Black queer people engage Black queer placemaking through performance. As a result, Blackness and queerness converge in public. During a humid midafternoon, Aaron—a queer femme from Tennessee—and I walk on Patchen Avenue toward Do the Right Thing Way to attend the 2019 block party, which is being hosted by Spike Lee. As we make our way toward Quincy Street, we notice a group of three Black men in their midthirties walking in our same direction on the opposite side of the street. I hear '90s hip-hop playing. "We must be gettin' close!" Aaron says with great excitement. Once we turn onto Quincy Street, we notice a group of three feminine-presenting Black men standing next to three metal chairs facing north toward the block party. The men are dancing together in a circle to the sound of the '90s hip-hop song blasting from the speakers. They move their hips to the right, then to the left, drop to the ground, and repeat. In the window of the apartment is a poster of civil rights activist Bayard Rustin (also known as "Mr. March on Washington"). Rustin (1912–87) was a Black openly gay socialist who organized a number of protests in the 1940s, 1950s, and 1960s, including the 1963 March on Washington for Jobs and Freedom, for which he was named deputy director (Carson et al. 1994). Unfortunately, Rustin was not given proper recognition for his efforts due to his sexual identity (Carson et al. 1994). A small black barbeque grill is directly behind the dancing men. White clouds of smoke emerge from the top of the grill and diffuse into the air. The strong smell of smoked hickory chips fills my nose and teases my sense of taste. As we walk closer to the block party, I notice well over one hundred people standing in front of a large stage. The crowd—mostly Black masculine and feminine-presenting people who range in age from early twenties to late sixties—are packed close together. A large red banner hangs on the left side of the stage with "Do The Right Thing" printed in white letters. A black banner with the Beats by Dr. Dre (2015) logo is printed across the top of the stage (see figure 1.3).

Black queer spatiality is a spatial happening. Black queer spatiality, for example, emerges on the corner of Quincy Street and Patchen Avenue by the

FIGURE 1.3. Do the Right Thing block party. Photograph by the author.

human activity at this location. First, consider the three Black femmes. The first femme is wearing a fringed, cropped white T-shirt and black jeans. The second has on a black mesh shirt and shorts, and the third has frayed denim shorts and a black bralette. The three Black femmes are making place by taking up literal space with their Black femme queer embodiment and marking the corner using objects such as a poster of Bayard Rustin in the street-facing apartment window. The placement of the Bayard Rustin poster in the window is an intentional Black queer political act that is a symbolic reminder of Black queer cultural histories in civil rights era protests, and the unabashed Black queer political exercise destabilizes heteronormativity in the block party, predominantly public Black space. Therefore, the Bayard Rustin poster transcends aesthetics and consumption; it signifies the presence of Black queer public culture—including histories of protest and lived experiences of Blackness and queerness—in and around Black spaces such as the block party. Political scientist and feminist Cathy J. Cohen (2005) contends that queer politics recognizes and supports the movement and fluidity of people's social lives. For example, the block party is an anniversary event celebrating a film about public resistance against anti-Black racism. Therefore, Black queer politics is demonstrated by the poster because it destabilizes heteronormativity and heterosexism through space.

E. Patrick Johnson (2001) introduced the term "quare" in his article "'Quare' Studies, or (Almost) Everything I Know about Queer Studies I Learned from My Grandmother." Later, Johnson and Mag G. Henderson (2005) encouraged scholars to challenge the traditional use of "queer" and highlight its intersection with Blackness by *quaring* queer:

> We want to *quare* queer—to throw shade on its meaning in the spirit of extending its service to "blackness." Further, we believe that there are compelling social and political reasons to lay claim to the modifier "black" in "black queer." Both terms, of course, are markers or signifiers of difference: just as "queer" challenges notions of heteronormativity and heterosexism, "black" resists notions of assimilation and absorption. And so we endorse the double cross of affirming the inclusivity mobilized under the sign of "queer" while claiming the racial, historical, and cultural specificity attached to the marker "black." (7)

This quote provides an intersectional framework for my conception and mobilization of "Black queer" in Black queer spatiality. Black queer spatiality signifies the cultural and historical legacies of Black people. Black queer spatiality as a theory thinks through how, why, and to what extent space is produced as extensions of people and is commodified, policed, and multidimensional relative to its social dimensions and characteristics. Furthermore, Black queer spatiality draws connections to materiality from spatial production, maintenance, and performance while also recognizing the critical involvement that immateriality has with space and people. Therefore, Black queer spatiality recognizes legacies and conditions of Black people while maintaining queerness at the center—it *quares* queer.

The three Black femmes dance to the hip-hop music at the block party. Their arms raised to the sky, their wrists flicking from side to side to the beat of "Juicy" by The Notorious B.I.G., they rap, "It was all a dream! I used to read 'Word Up' magazine!" Their bodies move intimately against one another, before each body breaks away from the others only to touch again. While in a circle, they move in closer and move out again as they rap along: "I'm blowin' up like you thought I would. Call the crib, same number, same hood. It's all good!" Their dance form is a distinctive activity that signifies a disassociation from Black heteronormativity that labels Black same-sex-loving people as deviant, even while dancing. Heteronormativity in the US requires people to engender a set of socially constructed social codes that disallow men from showing affection toward other men and women toward other women and support committing violence toward transgender people through, at best, intentionally misgendering them. As Audre Lorde (1984) reminds us, compulsory heterosexuality is understood by dominant society as normative; it is a practice of privilege, and any other form of human sexuality outside of heterosexuality or emotionality is aberrant, vile, or abnormal. Black heteronormativity reproduces narrow normative frames that the majority of US and Canadian societies internalize. As a result, Black heteronormativity oppresses and marginalizes Black LGBTQ people. Weslev Crichlow's (2004) *Buller Men and Batty Bwoys: Hidden Men in Toronto and Halifax Black Communities* discusses Black heteronormativity (Black first) in relation to the Black church, for example:

> For buller men and batty bwoys (Black gay men), the oppressions of racism, sexism, classism, and heterosexism are inextricably linked. Despite the different patterns that oppression takes, many of its machinations follow the "blame the victims" syndrome. All of these "isms" deny bullers and batty bwoys their human agency. They regulate, oppress, deny, and suppress the fantasies, differences, desires, and practices of bullers. The Black church, Black nationalism, and the Black family constitute the triple pillar that obstructs progress on the issue of Black same-sex loving. (26)

The dance form of the three Black femmes at the block party dismisses the social codes that dominant society engenders and maintains. Their bodies perform distinctive activities and imaginings associated with a particular place. The feminine-presenting bodies constitute race, class, and gender through Black queer imaginings. By Black queer imaginings, I mean the conception of a Black queer world (or Black queertopia) where their lived experiences occlude structures of power that reinforce normative sexuality. In addition, their Black queer imaginings, which are reflected in their body movements, hand gestures, and intimate dance form, upset Black heteronormativity, namely the block party, by creating an affirming place and inherent sociospatial meanings elsewhere.

"Should we squeeze by the straights and get a spot near the front? Or stand near the outside of the crowd?" Aaron asks. Aaron stops twenty feet away from the large crowd. "Well, let's stand here," he says. In the middle of the stage, we notice the DJ wearing khaki shorts and a white T-shirt. A microphone stand is next to him. The DJ's deep voice grabs everyone's attention as he says, "Y'all ready for this, Brooklyn?" Everyone in the crowd screams in response to the DJ's question, "Yes!"

Wayne Wonder's "No Letting Go" starts playing from the large sound system on the stage. I notice a tall, slender Black man and a Black women grab hands to begin dancing together. The man's green linen pants and white linen shirt blow in the wind. His dreadlocks sway from left to right as he moves his lower body from right to left. His body moves in an opposite direction to his hand movement. His body shifts to the left and his hand, which is locked into the woman's hand, moves to the right. The Black woman's long, orange dress flows against the wind as her body moves to the beat. Her voluminous afro is a big accessory that reflects her freedom and liberation.[3] Her gold Nefertiti necklace manages to rest against her chest despite her spirited dance moves. Most of the people who are standing near the stage collectively move to the beat of the song. "If you don't know how to dance, you will learn today!" a Black woman standing nearby exclaims. As the song continues, there are at least ten man-woman pairs dancing closely together to the beat of the music.

Aaron says with excitement, "I wish one of these Brooklyn men would come dance with me. *Snap!* "Get over here, brotha!" Aaron then turns to me and says, "I need one of these brothas to come to our corner." His arms gently move from left to right. His hips snap back and forth. "See, I been practicing." *Snap!* Once the song comes to an end, everyone in the crowd begins clapping as if to give themselves a standing ovation. *Snap!* The DJ returns to the mic and says, "Fellas, y'all got that special lady? Ladies, does your fella make you feel special?" Attempting to yell over the clapping, Aaron shouts, "Yes! My Brooklyn man right over there makes me feel special!" He points to the tall Black man with back-length dreadlocks. *Snap!*

Here, Aaron makes place, particularly Black queer place, at the outermost edge of the block party crowd. He queers the block party through a set of comprehensive actions. First, Aaron marks the area where we stand through snapping his fingers, a sociopolitical gesture of Black queerness engendered with nuances. For example, Black queer filmmaker and activist Marlon T. Riggs (2017) writes,

> The Snap! contains a multiplicity of coded meanings—as in SNAP! "Got your point!" or SNAP! "Don't even try it!" or SNAP! "You fierce!" or SNAP! "Get out my face!" or SNAP! "Girlfriend, pleeeease." The Snap! can be as emotionally and politically charged as a clenched fist; can punctuate debate and dialogue like an exclamation point, a comma, an ellipsis; or can altogether negate the need for words among those who are adept at decoding nuanced meanings. (784)

---

3. In December 2020, Connie Suggitt (2020) interviewed Simone Williams from Brooklyn, New York. Williams broke the world record for the largest afro (woman). Her afro is 20.5 centimeters (8.07 inches) tall, 22.5 centimeters (8.85 inches) wide, and 1.48 meters (4 feet and 10 inches) in circumference.

Place emerges through what people do, including the singular gestures of official marking. By official marking, I mean the act of labeling a place or marked place by using written text. However, marking place also includes bodily acts. Aaron's snaps are coded with geopolitical meanings, including race, gender, and place. First, Aaron's crisp snaps are directed toward the dancing crowd—showing a sense of balance—as well as his own movement. *Snap!* "This my song!" Secondly, Aaron's snaps create a boundary—bounded place—around the immediate area where we stand on the margins of the crowd. *Snap! Snap! Snap!* His hips move from side to side on beat to the music. The bounded place emerges as meanings of Black queerness—Aaron's passionate dance moves and the sounds of his crisp snaps, as well as his pronounced imaginary, where he and the other Black cisgender male are in a sexual partnership.

Historically, however, Black people's relationships to public and private space across the US have almost always been facilitated by institutions, from slavery to the Federal Housing Association. Black people's struggle through space necessitates spatial possibilities for the Black body. The block party, then, is a social formation; it is a spatial event that I refer to as a Black spatiality. Black spatiality demonstrates a set of spatial possibilities where Black people are affirmed through space and placemaking by naming a bounded place after a cultural production that acknowledged racial tension in Brooklyn. In addition to naming a street Do the Right Thing Way, place emerges. Place emerges at the new named street through the act of memorializing Black public culture that discusses histories and lived experiences that limited Black people's mobility and occluded Black public culture in New York City. In addition, Black public culture also recognizes histories of anti-Blackness in federal housing policy.

Implications of Federal Housing Policy on Black Homeownership

In the 1940s, federal housing policies in Richmond, California, predetermined residential spaces that Black people could occupy. Richard Rothstein (2017) discusses the ways in which public housing was rapidly constructed to house Black war workers. The quality of public housing for Black war workers was dilapidated at best due to the rate at which the public housing was developed. Rothstein (2017, 5) says, "with such rapid population growth, housing could not be put up quickly enough. The federal government stepped in with public housing. It was officially and explicitly segregated." Between 1940 and 1945, the Black population rose from 270 to 14,000. As if the segregation of housing facilities was not enough, Richmond police enforced rules developed by the housing authority for Black people who resided in public housing complexes. The housing authority designated particular hours during the day that Black people could use the recreational and sports facilities. Interracial gathering was not allowed. Therefore, public and private spaces in Richmond for Black people were predetermined, temporary, and intentionally segregated through legislation and interpersonal bias. As a whole, space was used as a vector of power to control Black people, which, in turn, had detrimental effects at various levels of felt intensities.

In a similar vein, from the onset of World War II to 1955, the housing authority in New York City constructed twenty large unsubsidized projects for middle-class families who paid rent that covered the housing costs. Many projects across New York City were attractive low-rise developments, with trees, grassy areas, and park benches. Although priority was given to veterans, the housing authority maintained a list of twenty-one disqualifying factors for prospective tenants, including irregular employment history, single-parent family or an out-of-wedlock birth, criminal record, narcotic addiction, mental illness, poorly behaved children, poor housekeeping habits, and lack of sufficient furniture.

These rules were racially coded. They were developed to keep Black people from fully integrating public housing projects. Rothstein (2017, 18) adds that to ensure undesirable tenants were not accepted, the housing authority sent agents to inspect the condition in which applicants kept their previous homes, often shared with relatives. Thus purchasing, occupying, and maintaining space, either public or private, in Richmond or New York, were processes that were in tandem with discriminatory housing policies handed down by the federal government as an attempt to protect whiteness (property), minimize interracial recreational activities, and institute a social order that placed Black people toward the bottom. The history of segregation goes back before the period explored by Rothstein (2017). An additional example can be found in Chicago. The felt consequences of questionable Chicago politics through the early 1900s and beyond include constructing neighborhoods based on race and class. Davarian L. Baldwin's (2009) "Mapping the Black Metropolis: A Cultural Geography of the Stroll" discusses Chicago's Black Belt. The Black Belt was an area—a Black neighborhood—stretching from Eighteenth Street to Thirty-Ninth Street and bounded by State Street on the east and the Rock Island Railroad tracks and LaSalle Street on the west. Most public institutions and private academic institutions understood that their operating and financial status relied on Chicago's politicians and their political strategies. At this time, Black businesses were restricted to Eighteenth to Thirty-Ninth Streets (the South Side) (Baldwin 2009). Because extracting wealth for the sake of accumulating white wealth is the American way, Black people were steered from homeownership in white areas by the Hyde Park–Kenwood Property Owners Association in the early 1900s (Baldwin 2009). The basic and anti-Black reason for their practice: to protect property values from the contamination from a person of color.

Considering Black people have struggled over and through public and private space, the block party is a site of encounter in Brooklyn's public sphere. The block party happens in public space to commemorate a street named after a film about racial tension. The music, stage performances, and audience performances allow Blackness to be understood, sited, and celebrated in Do the Right Thing Way—a bounded space. Blackness is sensed by the block party attendees, envelops Do the Right Thing Way, and provokes nostalgia for places marked by Blackness. Place emerged as a result of naming a portion of Lexington Avenue Do the Right Thing Way. Yet I want to explore the ways in which Black queerness does not appear at the margins, but where it is centered, wholly.

"Let's Go Out to Langston's"

On June 30, 2019, I receive a phone call from Aaron at 9:30 p.m. Aaron, who I attended the block party with, moved to Brooklyn after earning a degree from Brown University. Before I could say "hi" he asks, "Whatchu doin' tonight? You know you ain't doin' nothin'! Let's go out to Langston's! It's close to you and you won't have to take the subway." "What time?" I respond. "Around midnight, sus." I hesitate and say, "Okay, I'll meet you there around midnight, okay?" When we arrive, there are two Black femmes speaking to each other while on their way out. "So, what he said, sus?" I overhear one of the femmes say to the other.

Note the gesture of kinship: saying "sus" demonstrates a close-knit familial relationship, and a complex system of friendship and kinship networks in community social order are reflected in this example. Marlon M. Bailey's (2013) *Butch Queens up in Pumps* is an ethnography of Ballroom culture that explains the ways in which space is socially produced and the extent to which subjectivities (gender and sexual categories) are claimed, packaged, and performed. Bailey's work demonstrates how Black queer individuals have challenged hegemonic masculinity and tropes of racialized gender by forging subjectivities in spaces of care and racialized gender such as that of the ballroom.

Ballroom, as Bailey (2013) demonstrates, is a place insofar as it is marked by converging subjective experiences of the Black and Latino individuals who inhabit it. Yet social places marked by Black queer individuals such as the ballroom, club, bar, or bathhouse are being squeezed out to guarantee the flow of capital. As Bailey (2013) explains, Ballroom members—who forge new possibilities of kinship—conceive, perform, and concretize subjectivities that expand the gender categories of the majoritarian sphere or public sphere as well as the notion of kinship in radical ways. As another example, consider a text message I received from D, a shorter Black gay man who recently moved to Atlanta to continue his work in public health. "Hey, kween! Whatchu doin'?" I responded, "Out and about, diva!" I was not actually out in public, but I was away from my home completing my research fieldwork. D calls me "queen" to form a royal kinship structure and relationship between the two of us. D's text message is a new mode of resistance that destabilizes normative family and gender systems.

I met D in high school, and we used to walk around the mall and J-Sette. J-Setting is a popular southern dance style that is akin to the Jackson State University Sonic Boom of the South marching band women's dance line. D and I met at the Father of the House of Malone in Mobile, Alabama, at Mardi Gras 2008—which was my first time hearing about Ballroom and house cultures. The following year, while on break from our predominantly white and racist boarding school in Mobile, we offered to drive a group of the house members to downtown Prichard, Alabama, to go to a Black gay bar called Rainbow Lounge (known colloquially as Rainbow's). We knew nothing about Rainbow's prior to meeting this group, and we did not know that Prichard had gay people, let alone a gay gathering spot. We drove them to Prichard since I had access to my mom's Buick at the time and we wanted to hang out. We needed a fun night after weeks of submitting college applications, so why not? We also wanted to see for ourselves that Prichard had a gay spot. Prichard is a predominantly Black area (according to the 2020 census data, Prichard's Black population is 85 percent). Prichard—located just outside of Mobile—witnessed disinvestment and uneven development, and it is where I actually grew up and realized firsthand the consequences of uneven development and disinvestment. D would later go to Auburn University and then Morehouse College. Since high school we have remained in contact, remembering Rainbow's and the Black LGBTQ people we befriended.

Some time later, D texted me and asked, "You remember we drove to Montgomery for First Wednesday, gay night?"

"Yeah, I remember that."

D said, "I remember we walked in and there was some fine ass pretty boys everywhere! There was some of everybody up in there. Whew, that was long ago! Damn. I used to leave there with sweat dripping off my chin. I would be on the dance floor shaking my ass and looking for someone to tickle me!"

I chuckled and said, "Yeah, you and me both!"

"So, wassup tonight?" he asked.

"Well, I'm going out to a Black gay spot here in Brooklyn in a bit and I have to get ready," I said with excitement.

"Okay, then I'll hit you up later."

We hung up. I opened a house music mix on my SoundCloud phone application and turned it up because I had the apartment to myself.

Spatial Re/Configuring + Black Queer Placemaking

Considering my aunt will be gone for the night, I produce Black queer spatiality and exercise my agency as a Black queer in her absence. After I decide on an outfit, I move my aunt's tan-colored sofa bed against her white dining room wall. After that, I slide her glass coffee table against the eastern wall of the living room. As a result of the spatial configuration, I create an area within my aunt's apartment that allows me to FaceTime Aaron and show him what I will be wearing to Langston's. "Hey, sus! Is that what you wearin'? Ohh! Let's get tickled by the brothas tonight!" He starts dancing in the frame of the camera. I can tell he has produced his own Black queer spatiality with a higher intensity than my own. "It's All about Me" by Mya playing in the background, coupled with Aaron's sense of balance as he dances, are dimensions of his Black queer spatiality. His Black queer spatiality yields spatial articulations including race and gender that I can ultimately sense. For example, Mya's song that plays in the background frames his Blackness that is predicated on queerness. Blackness and queerness are converging as he dances because he performs femininity through dance and expresses his desire to be "tickled" by a "brotha" tonight. I produce Black queer spatiality by moving objects in my aunt's apartment and FaceTiming Aaron, who is *quaring* queer.

I produce Black queer spatiality in the context of my spatial imaginary, which is motivated by Black queer livability, histories, and expressions—a Black queer space that provides me with a field of possibilities and conditions that allows me to do all that I intend to do: interrupt normativity through bodily acts. I repeatedly scurry from the small, bright bathroom into the living room trying on outfits and checking myself in the bathroom mirror. I lay two outfit choices across the tan living room sofa to visualize what I'll wear to Langston's before trying them on.

My first choice of an outfit is blue jeans, a black T-shirt, and white and black sneakers. My second choice is black denim jeans and a mesh top. I decide to wear blue jeans, a black V-neck T-shirt, and black Vans with white accents. I want to "fit in." I reflect on a conversation I had with Marcus, a Dominican and Haitian man in his early thirties, about "fitting in." He said:

> Pre-gentrified Brooklyn was a Brooklyn that I was always idealistic about but also a Brooklyn that I was also trying to resist and desperately escape. It makes me uncomfortable to say this, but this is now home in the truest sense of the word. It's home now because of the safety and habitability that gentrification has brought on. I'm anchored here. And because I'm anchored here, I have intentionally sought out spaces that can both accommodate my Blackness and my queerness. A gentrified Brooklyn allows that for me.

Marcus describes fitting in as a mechanism, practice, or hegemonic process, such as gentrification, that allows him to feel comfortable. Comfortability refers to Marcus's ability to feel at ease in the spaces he moves through and occupies. Yet gentrification in Atlanta, for example, is erasing Black identity in some areas. Doan and Higgins (2011) examine the effects of gentrification on LGBTQ neighborhoods in Atlanta, Georgia, causing the erasure of Blackness. The areas that were predominantly LGBTQ include Midtown, Candler Park, Decatur, North DeKalb County, South DeKalb County, East Atlanta, and East Point. Doan and Higgins (2011) found that gentrification had a significant effect on LGBTQ neighborhoods in Atlanta.

Gentrification has consistently caused LGBTQ neighborhoods such as Midtown in Atlanta to struggle to maintain LGBTQ and Black identities. LGBTQ neighborhoods—read as white—are overwhelmingly corporatized and commercialized. Black LGBTQ people and culture are underrepresented and underprotected in public spaces at the neighborhood level. However, aspects of Black LGBTQ public culture like music and dance are commodified to further substantiate LGBTQ neighborhood commercialization. Therefore, Black queer people rely on places such as Langston's to resist cisgender white heteronormativity and perform care-work. Black queer people also intentionally articulate Blackness and queerness in space to perform care-work and represent the Black LGBTQ public culture that commodification attempts to co-opt.

Spatial articulations are a humanistic social scientific concept that identifies marked elements, spatial interactions, and sensations that are unique to a particular place and time; spatial articulations describe its sense of place, in part. For example, Black queerness is a social identity and a spatial articulation following intentional action and interaction. Moreover, spatial articulations function as systems of sociospatial power to destabilize structures of anti-Blackness and Black heteropatriarchy and the normative race, gender, and sexual ideologies that undergird them through inter/personal spatial acts. The atmosphere that I observe during Aaron's FaceTime demonstrates an upbeat, Black queer atmosphere.

Historical thinkers inspire contemporary ideas. Conceptualizations and theorizations regarding atmosphere have been inspired by Karl Marx (1978), who argues that atmosphere envelops and presses on social life. Moreover, Anderson (2009) is influenced by the phenomenology of aesthetic experience described by Mikel Dufrenne (1953). According to Anderson (2009, 79), "atmospheres are perpetually forming and deforming, appearing and disappearing, as bodies enter in relation with one another. They are never finished, static or at rest." In a sense, Anderson (2009) is alluding to the spatiotemporal and kinesthetic aspects regarding movement, bodies, and atmospheres. To put this differently, Anderson (2009) wants geographers and social actors who produce space, make place, and create atmospheres to understand that atmosphere is almost always changing and becoming, depending on the bodies that are producing the space. Taking this further, atmospheres have both subjective and objective qualities that are felt (emotional) and pre-personal (affective). According to German philosopher Gernot Böhme (1993),

> atmospheres are neither something objective, that is, qualities possessed by things, and yet they are something thinglike, belonging to the thing in that things articulate their presence through qualities—conceived as ecstasies. Nor are atmospheres something subjective, for example determinations of a psychic state. And yet they are subjectlike, belong to subjects in that they are sense in bodily presence by human beings and this sensing is at the same time a bodily state of being of subjects in space. (122)

Therefore, atmospheres are thing-like and subject-like. After talking and listening to the old-school '90s R&B song through FaceTime for few minutes, Aaron says, "We have to go! Let's get off and go down to Langston's!" I recognize Aaron's Black queer spatiality through the interface of the cell phone and through its capacity to effect nostalgia, or longing for a 1990s moment in time. Nostalgia, to return to the formulation of Kitson and McHugh (2015, 490), "is a lively, pre-personal affect which registers in and through the sensory contact of bodies and things." Although this is from the vantage point of new materialisms, this perspective of nostalgia is one that relies on a capacity to affect and be affected. Taking this further, nostalgia is realized when bodies are oriented in a certain direction, especially under conditions of the horizon.

After walking out of the elevator, I turn right and head for the exit to Claremont Avenue. While passing the building's doorman, Alfonso, he yells to me, "Hey, bro!" I stop and turn to have a conversation. Alfonso is a thirty-something Dominican man with a daughter. He's about five feet nine with short black hair. For my birthday, he had gone out of his way to buy me a cupcake and sing to me while he was on the clock. He writes music and often plays his guitar in the lobby.

Alfonso asks with excitement, "Where you headed? I wrote a new song and I want you to hear it."

I turn to him and say, "I'm going to Langston's in Brooklyn. I want to see what's going on there tonight."

He replies, "Oh yeah? I been there, but don't tell nobody. I wanna keep it under wraps."

I smile and say, "I hear you."

"You know if my baby mama found out that I was there, she would have a field day. You know I already don't see my baby girl as much as I need to. You see this music thing gotta work out for me. It'll be good for us."

I say, "Yeah, I hear you. How was Langston's when you were there? Did you enjoy your time there?" He laughs and says,

> Yeah, I did. You know it was cool. I was mostly looking at the guys, vibin' and listening to the music. The music was on point. The hip-hop music was really good, and you know I was getting inspired by the music and I wanted to get on the mic and sing some things I had wrote some days before I went there. I really wanted to. You know I'm fly and I wanted to show off my music and show the fellas I got it too. You know?

I reply, "You didn't get up there? Why not?" He looks down to the floor and says,

> Well, you have to have some confidence. The guys in there are expecting talent, confidence, and a show. In my head, I would have the whole place singing with me. Instead, I was singing and dancing with myself and looking at the guys walk by of course. Plus, I didn't want to be recorded or anything because my baby mama would find out. I'm real protective that way. I want to see my daughter.

I say, "I understand. Well, I hope to hear your song when I get back from Langston's."

He laughs and says, "Yeah, I'll be here. You know I'm here all night. When you get back, I want you to hear my song and I want your honest opinion. Okay?"

"Okay, I got you," I say. I turn to walk out of the apartment building. I turn right onto Claremont Avenue and begin walking to Langston's.

After walking for a few minutes, I sense sounds and smells of Blackness. The sounds of Blackness include soulful rhythms that are unique to the Black diaspora. The lyrics that are categorized as Black music discuss the current and historic conditions of Black people around the world. The smells of Blackness refer to the unique spices used in Jamaican cuisine, such as cloves, thyme, Scotch bonnet peppers, and garlic. My sense of a Black space is contextualized as my senses of sight and smell confirm it. For example, I notice a group of fifteen Black people who range in age from childhood to middle age outside of the Nigerian American Muslim Integrated Community Center. The building itself resembles a large brown fortress. Outside of the building, I notice some Black women who don bright blue dresses and others yellow. However, all of the Black men are dressed in black suits. Then, I catch a unique smell that permeates the street. The smell of food is hypnotizing to me, and I want to understand what is happening nearby. Therefore, I take a detour. I cross onto the other side of Clermont Avenue and walk north toward Willoughby. Clermont Avenue is quintessential Brooklyn—peppered with wide brown steps leading up to brownstones. The avenue is also lined by a number of established trees. I notice a group of three Black women in deep conversation. One woman in particular starts clapping her hands and jumping while conversing with the other two women.

I hear someone say, "Yes, brother!" My eyes shift to a tall Black man speaking to another Black man who is of equal height. Kids' laughter becomes increasingly louder as I continue to slowly walk north on Clermont Avenue. I see young Black children dressed in black pants and white oxford shirts. The smell of food intensifies as I get closer. Then, I see a white banner reading "Ramadan" on the front of the association.

It is after midnight by the time I make it to Langston's. I notice a line of fifteen Black men lined up to get in. I am dressed the part. Some men have on dark-wash jeans and T-shirts while others wear white shorts with polo shirts tucked in. "Hey, sus!" my friend yells to me, and I join him in line. As we wait, the bass line of Janet Jackson's "Control" shakes the sidewalk under our feet. It is just past midnight and a group of three Black men who are in their mid- to late thirties climb out of a cab and run up to another group of Black thirty-somethings who stand near the entrance and are also waiting to get inside of Langston's. One man wears dark jeans, a white and navy oxford shirt, and a gray fedora hat. The other two men are dressed similarly in light-colored slim linen cotton shorts and black mesh T-shirts.

"Oh, chile! How long y'all been waitin'?" one clubgoer says to the other.

"Not long, chile," the other person in line mumbles.

"Ohhhhh! You look good, Q! Who husband you finna steal tonight, chile?" the first clubgoer says in true shady fashion.

To which the second responds, "You messy as hell . . . but my neighbor husband if he lucky!"

"Next!" the club bouncer says to us. I reach into my pocket and hand him my ID and he tells me to pay inside. I walk inside to a dark foyer with a black sheet fashioned to divide the bar from the pay area. The Black woman behind the counter says, "Twenty dollars." I reach into my pocket and handed her a twenty-dollar bill. "Thank you, sweetness," she says as she reaches for my money. I smile and proceed to walk inside to the dimly lit bar area to the right.

Cover charges have become the norm in most spaces, including night-clubs, bars, and live music venues. It is important to note that cover charges act as a way to accumulate revenue, cover operational costs (security, maintenance, and entertainment), deter unwanted guests to ensure that a target audience is maintained, and control crowd size inside the venue (FasterCapital 2023). At Langston's, the cover charge serves as a way to screen patrons who may not visit Langston's with the same intentions as its general patrons. Therefore, cover charges are a barrier to filter guests so that patrons will enjoy a pleasant atmosphere rather than a chaotic atmosphere. For example, if Langston's did not have a cover charge, the chances of people who would change the desired atmosphere in Langston's would likely increase, and by extension, the likelihood of a nonqueer person causing a disturbance would increase.

In addition to screening people before entering Langston's in order to decrease the likelihood that its desired atmosphere is compromised, the lounge's cover charge places barriers for Black queer people who desire to access Langston's who have lower socioeconomic means. At Langston's I notice Black men wearing designer hats, shoes, and shirts. My observation coupled with the cover charge suggests that the cover charge makes Langston's an exclusive space that is made available for Black queer people who have the means to pay for entrance and entertainment while inside the lounge. In other words, the cover charge is meant to deter cash-poor Black queer people from entering.

The inside is dark, and the only light comes from blue, red, and white strobe lights from three corners of the bar. Black men line the wall of the bar to the left. They appear to be in their early thirties. They wear fitted baseball hats and trucker hats to the back and dark sneakers, as well as white T-shirts. They stand like statues. The dance floor is packed with young Black men who wear white shorts and skintight tank tops in a variety of colors dancing to "Too Good" by Drake featuring Rihanna.

We make our way to the center of the packed dance floor and dance to the rest of the song. As we dance, the blue and green lights shine against our bodies and the interior walls of the bar. As we dance, my arm touches the damp hand of the thirtysomething-year-old man next to me. He does not say anything, nor do I. Langston's atmosphere is unique to this space and the Black people within it. It is queer, it is Black, it is a Black queer community. It is at that point that I consider the material elements, including the cocktail tables, plastic cocktail cups, large black stereo speakers, and centrally located silver disco ball, and immaterial elements, including the feeling of the bass beat under my feet, the heat that causes sweat to run down my back, and the performances that form and characterize a Black queer bar. The foundation upon which Black LGBTQ culture and personhood rests heavily shifts away from public spaces that include heteronormative social interactions. By this I mean Black LGBTQ people and culture unfold in nonnormative spaces due to the threat of commodification and co-optation from non-Black LGBTQ people. However, my interest in a publicly private world such as Langston's calls into question the impact of queer placemaking and its significance to Black queer people across Brooklyn and beyond. In what follows, I chart my own spatial story about Langston's by identifying sensuous geographies, particularly Black queer spatial experiences, to provide a critical understanding of Black queer sense of place, largely. Black queer spatiality is a comprehensive two-part spatial exercise that describes sensuous geographies and spatial articulations. First, Black queer spatiality involves identifying Black queer sociopolitical spatial performances that are unique to temporary Black queer social sites. One example of Black queer sociopolitical spatial performance includes an interruption in the flow of things in a dedicated area conceived by urban planners and architects. More specifically, Black queer spatiality involves resistance practices; it is where race, gender, and sexuality are spatially articulated. Take, for instance, the ways in which the West Side piers were reimagined by queers as a cruising spot for sex in the '70s and '90s. Now, Christopher Street Pier has been renovated for newcomers who have complained against the noise from the nearby gay bars and clubs. Yet Black queer youth who are a part of the Kiki scene continue to lay claim to Christopher

Street Pier to this day. The Kiki scene is a subset of the house and Ballroom scene; it is a community of LGBTQ youth of color, predominantly Black and Latinx youth, and the focus is on youth development and community networking (Jordenö 2016). Vogue performance in the Kiki scene takes place in public. Often, members of the Kiki scene vogue around a large group of Black LGBTQ people who clap, snap, and yell, "Yass, kween!" and scream, "Boww!" as they perform what is called a "death drop." A death drop is a dance move that involves falling backward onto the ground at the end of the dance. The death drop is an exclamation point on a performer's entire performance. Therefore, vogue performance is a resistance practice that is supported by the dancers' Kiki family by interrupting the normative social codes that are inherent in dominant space.

Following this, Black queer spatiality requires critical analysis of identity, performance, and sensation, and at times, nostalgia in and across a geographic site. Thus, Black queer spatiality relies on active and/or remembered spatial dimensions and happenings that are akin to places occupied by Black queer people. Black queer spatiality is an approach that enables both social policy and academic circles to prioritize the interplay between race, class, gender, sexuality, and space such that land-use policies can be reconfigured to support Black queer spatial agency and representation. The point is that Black queer spatiality provides space, opportunity, and a sense of belonging that the world does not extend to racial and sexual minorities.

On another visit to Langston's, I quickly make my way to the front entrance. "You have really good eye contact," the Black woman behind the counter tells me. I give her twenty dollars, then proceed behind the black drape to enter the club. The '90s R&B song "My Boo" by Ghost Town DJ's is blasting through the speakers. The bass line is felt under my feet. There are five Black men wearing denim shorts and V-neck T-shirts dancing in the middle of the bar under the silver disco ball. I make my way to the bar and order a cocktail, squeezing between men and women who are lining the outside of the dance floor. I lock eyes with a Black man in his early thirties. He is wearing a long-sleeve white oxford shirt, jeans, and brown loafers. His locs are braided up and rest on his head like a crown. He smiles at me and I smile back. I finally find a spot against the bar, and I order a drink. While I'm waiting, I notice several small plastic cups on top of the bar, napkins thrown haphazardly across the bar top, and receipts piling up to the right of the cash register. The fog machine is not turned on yet, but the smell of fresh-cut grass and wood is in the air from the wood fixtures and sweating bodies inside of Langston's.

As I wait for the tatted bartender to make my drink, I notice two men grinding up against each other and mouthing the words of the song, "I need you, I want you, to have you, hold you, squeeze you. So, I'm going out every weekend, just to see my Boo again." I start singing along to the song. The red, green, and blue neon lights, the only lights in the bar, move around the room. The two men who are grinding take their drinks and move to the dance floor, the shorter man in front of the taller man grinding as best he can while moving toward the dance floor.

As a space, the Black queer bar is an environment that serves as a social alternative to Black cisgender heteropatriarchal spaces. As a place, Langston's is a locale where social identities and social interactions are embedded in space; it is a site of queer performative specificities. Black queer spatiality is a theory and a method that prioritizes atmosphere (McGlotten 2014; Anderson 2009; Burgin 1998; McHugh 2009), nostalgia (Farrar 2011), and sensations (Anderson 2009) as critical dimensions of spatial experience that build theoretical foundations of spatial knowledge that center Black queer people's spatial experience.

Atmospheres become through the social interactions and encounters within a space's marked spatial boundaries—the boundary between an interior and exterior. Also, atmospheres manifest through the ways in which attitudes and values are exchanged within the space. Think of how energies and intensities between bodies are felt rather than traced or mapped.

"What you drinkin' on, handsome?" the bartender asks me. He is a middle-aged, dark-skinned Black man who stands approximately five feet ten, wearing a white and blue tank top and blue shorts. I lean over the mahogany bar to tell him with a raised voice because the music drowns out my request the first time. As he pours my cocktail, I notice his right arm is covered in a tattoo of roses, his left arm has tattoos of four names, and his chest tattoo reads "BK," which is centered and in the same font as his other large tattoos. He hands me a small clear plastic cup and winks at me. I hand him my debit card to pay the twelve dollars for my cocktail. He then returns my card with a receipt and a blue ballpoint pen. He winks at me again. I smile and walk toward my friend who is standing impatiently near the dance floor. I take one sip of the cocktail through the small, black cocktail straw. I taste more whiskey than Sprite from the small plastic cup.

Spatial articulations happen when identity markers such as race, gender, and sexuality are recognized in space. My exchange with the bartender was characterized by queer desire. Queer desire is a mode of queer politics that is a critique of normative Western gender and sexual ideologies; queer desire is a politics practiced by queer people. Natalie Oswin (2008) provides a critical reading of "queer," disclosing notions and disputes that "queer" exists singularly or is a monolithic practice and notion that is practiced by an entire group of people; it is also a politics that critiques the ways in which space is produced as a desexualized material reality. That is, Oswin (2008) defines queer space as a space that offers a radical alternative to heterosexual space (a Western conception of space). Therefore, Black queer spatiality traces social relations that are not predicated on heteronormativity, but homoerotic and homonormative gestures in and across queer space.

Moreover, in the extent to which the two Black male-presenting bodies grind against each other, Blackness and queerness are spatially articulated. Thus, the spatial articulation is recognized and identified as queer interaction. Furthermore, spatial articulations upend basic (normative) notions of sex, gender, and sexuality; they are almost always in a process of becoming since people are almost always in a process of becoming in relation to other people in space.

According to Sarah Ahmed (2008, 52), "The relation between action and space is hence crucial. It is not simply that we act in space; spatial relations between subjects and others are produced through actions, which make some things available to be reached. Or, as Lefebvre suggests: 'Activity in space is restricted by that space; space "decides" what actually may occur, but even this "decision" has limits placed upon it.'"

Therefore, the space of Langston's is made relational through the social relations and processes that are exclusive to this space. For example, perhaps the objects in Langston's, which include photographs of James Baldwin and Bayard Rustin, or the sounds of 1980s house music by Todd Terry and Phuture, render some association with Langston's that cannot be rendered elsewhere. This is due to a host of reasons, including the music playlist, the posters on the walls, the smell of the space, the selection of cocktails that are available, and the material (e.g., plastic or glass) the cocktails are served in. These spatial elements, along with bodies in the space and their attitudes, characterize a space, manifesting its atmosphere. Sara Ahmed (2008) writes,

> The language here implies that bodies provide us with a tool, as that through which we "hold" or "grasp" onto things, but elsewhere Merleau-Ponty suggests that the body is not itself an instrument but a form of expression, a making visible of our intentions (1964: 5). What makes bodies different is how they inhabit space: space is not a container for the body; it does not contain the body as if the body were "in it." Rather bodies are submerged, such that they become the space they inhabit; in taking up space, bodies

move through space and are affected by the "where" of that movement. It is through this movement that the surface of spaces as well as bodies takes shape. (53)

Therefore, bodies are oriented toward the aesthetics, materiality, enchantment, and sensual urbanism achieved that is exclusive to Langston's. Taking this further, the bodies and other materialities that are associated with Langston's move through other bodies and affect them in ways that are fulfilling to the patrons' consciousness. Think about the way your body is affected by your favorite sweater or your childhood photo. There may or may not be a type of affectual response that is experienced through your body. Consider the contention of Ahmed (2008) as she discusses photographs on the wall and how they impact people who occupy the space:

Covering the walls . . . are photographs. The wedding photograph. Underneath are the family pictures, some formal (taken by photographers) and others more casual. The photographs are objects on the wall. They turn the wall into an object, something to be apprehended; something other than the edge of the room. And yet the wall in its turn disappears as an edge insofar as we apprehend the objects on its surface. Everywhere I turn, even in the failure of memory, reminds me of how the family home puts objects on display that measure sociality in terms of the heterosexual gift. (89–90)

When we compare wedding photographs with the photographs of Black literary geniuses such as James Baldwin that are affixed to the walls of Langston's, a certain orientation toward queer Black history reflects a type of spatiality in terms of the queer gaze, which is reified as the capacity to sense and be affected is realized. In the next chapter, I discuss world-making and explain the practices involved in Black queer placemaking.

Conclusion

This chapter has defined Black queer spatiality and explored how race, gender, and sexuality are spatialized at varying scales and intensities. I define Black queer spatiality as a spatial happening that contains many social relationships. Therefore, Black queer spatiality is socially produced by Black queer people with respect to their relationship to buildings, their relationships with others in and across buildings, and their atmospheric, nostalgic, and sensational attunements at the interstitial sites where their relationships collide. My explanation of Black queer spatiality was supported by my ethnographic field notes and landscape images taken while in Downtown Brooklyn. I mobilized ethnography as a method to analyze Black queer spatiality. Using my ethnographic field notes, I identified and explained how and to what extent my shared apartment in Brooklyn, a mosque in Fort Greene, Brooklyn's downtown, the Fort Greene neighborhood, and Langston's Brooklyn are important sites for Black queer spatiality at multiple scales.

CHAPTER 2

Starlite, the Warehouse, and Langston's

In the summer of 2019, I interviewed Milton, an older Black gay man who currently lives in Clinton Hill, Brooklyn, and teaches at the New School in New York City. He is also a consultant on the show *Pose*.[1] In the early 2000s, Milton served in a leadership role in People of Color in Crisis (POCC), a now-defunct Black LGBTQ community-based organization in Brooklyn. According to Milton, POCC was instrumental in organizing Black Pride—an annual event to increase Black LGBTQ visibility and provide resources to the Black LGBTQ community. Milton said, "We had a dance floor, free food, tents with housing and health-related resources, HIV testing, and even celebrities to headline the event. We booked Kelly Price one year. It was like our place." POCC produced a community of care that provided distinct resources for Black LGBTQ people, food, drinks, and free health screenings.

POCC's Black Pride provided space for Black LGBTQ people to see and engage one another; it was a self-affirming and public-facing celebration. Milton suggested that Black Pride provided space for Black LGBTQ people outside of clubs. He expressed dismay about the many Black gay clubs and "nights" in the Bronx, Queens, and Brooklyn that have closed. He shouted in his Brooklyn accent, "See, we had all these nights! You know we only get

---

1. *Pose* is a drama series set in the 1980s and '90s and highlights New York City's Ballroom culture.

a night. One night. One! How we supposed to check in with our people? See who doing who!" Here Milton is speaking to the vanishing Black LGBTQ clubs across Brooklyn (historic and current) and limitations on Black LGBTQ cultural nights. The limited times that Black LGBTQ people are more willing to attend hip-hop or house music nights also limits the time Black LGBTQ people can engage one another—as Milton said, to "see who is doing who." Thus, this chapter is about the many Black LGBTQ bars and clubs that have closed and how Black queer people engage in Black queer placemaking practices to resist their spatial marginalization and produce alternative, affirming sites. I argue that Black queer people engage in distinct activities to make place.

In the previous chapter, I drew from my own spatial experiences as I moved through Bedford-Stuyvesant to attend the Do the Right Thing block party and Downtown Brooklyn to visit now-shuttered Club Langston. I investigated Black queer people's placemaking practices. I outlined Black queer spatiality by focusing on what Black queer people do in public space, paying close attention to performance, sensation, and nostalgia. In this chapter, I discuss how Black queer people engage in Black queer placemaking practices. I introduce the concept of world-making as an analytic to describe Black queer placemaking, an act of making Black queer place. I use world-making to analyze values and qualities that are significant to Black queer people and their repetitious practices. For example, world-making is an intentional Black queer practice that disassociates from systems that oppress Black queer people such as anti-Black racism. Therefore, world-making provides a framework to analyze and destabilize such systems; it is a prerequisite for Black queer placemaking. In other words, world-making is an analytic to produce space differently, and Black queer placemaking is the practice of producing place. Black queer spatiality refers to the relationship between the senses that are produced and recognized by Black queer placemaking.

This chapter has three objectives. First, I will focus on the histories of displacement/extraction and spatial subjectivities that Black queer spatiality makes clear. By focusing on the histories of Black queer displacement in Brooklyn, I bring into focus the significance of Black queer space. Second, I discuss the sociohistorical conditions that necessitate Langston's, paying close attention to spatial articulations of anti-Blackness, homophobia, economic deprivation, and spatial segregation due to histories of Black queer displacement. Third, I discuss Black queer placemaking and world-making by focusing on what Black queer people do in Langston's, focusing primarily on gesturing, speaking, naming, and "gettin' yo' life"; world-making, then, is an analytic to understand what people do in Langston's. Together, these objectives suggest that Black queer placemaking is an act that resists the institutionalization and normalization of anti-Blackness, homophobia, economic deprivation, and spatial segregation. World-making is a fundamental practice for Black queer people to exercise their agency and engage in practices that dominant society defames. In the subsequent paragraphs, I discuss historic Black queer places.

Gettin' Yo' Life in Historic Black Queer Places

Starlite

Another Black LGBTQ bar that closed was the Starlite Lounge, which was located at 1084 Bergen Street in Crown Heights, Brooklyn. In 1962 (pre-Stonewall), Starlite was purchased by Harold "Mackie" Harris, an openly gay Black entrepreneur (Durkin 2011). In the 1950s, Crown Heights was 89 percent white, and by the early 1960s the Black population was approximately 25,000. At this time, Starlite was a neighborhood bar located in Crown Heights that attracted many Black people, straight and LBGTQ. Starlite was Black-owned at a time when there were not many Black people in the neighborhood. On Thursdays, karaoke nights were attended by straight and LGBTQ people. The crowd was multiracial (Urban Areas 2011). At 3 p.m., during the week, you could find mostly Black straight older men in the bar and Mama Dot bartending, sitting at the bar speaking with the long-term bargoers who had been visiting for thirty to forty years (Durkin 2011). Therefore, Starlite functioned differently for different groups of people at certain times. What people did in Starlite motivated its functionality.

Starlite was a significant place for Black queer people in Crown Heights and elsewhere in Brooklyn, especially from Friday to Sunday. On Fridays, Starlite held drag shows attended by mostly Black LGBTQ neighborhood regulars. On Saturdays, house music attracted Black gay men to Starlite from 11 p.m. to 2 a.m. On Sundays, Black LGBTQ people would dance the night away to house music mixed with old school R&B music. From 1992 to 2004, Starlite was owned by William "Butch" King, a DJ, who made Starlite a prime destination for house music (NYC LGBT Historic Sites Project 2017). After Butch's death in 2004, his sister, Linda King, inherited the bar (Dominus 2010).

Starlite was more than a neighborhood bar or a watering hole. The bar provided space for Black and Black LGBTQ people to sing karaoke, dance, "hook up," and participate and perform in drag shows. Starlite, then, was a community of care, considering the types of performances that were celebrated and the extent to which people were affirmed by seeing themselves and their culture within its walls.

Starlite was forced to close on Saturday, July 31, 2010. A large crowd of people showed up on the closing night—there was a line to get inside that stretched out of the entrance. The extensive entrance line demonstrates the level of appreciation for Starlite, a bar that provided a place where Black queer people could exercise their agency. In addition, there was a protest to save Starlite—a historical Black queer place, a community of care for Black and Black queer people in Crown Heights. Moreover, manager Tim La'Viticus made plans to obtain a lease renewal in court to fight for the reopening of the bar. Unfortunately, the building—built in 1920—was sold and the owner demanded that the bar vacate so repairs on the building could begin (Dominus 2010). A small convenience store replaced Starlite. As a result of the extraction of Black queer people and Black queer public culture, Black queer world-making and placemaking are necessary in order to preserve Black queer legacies and maintain representation.

The Warehouse

The Warehouse was located on East 140th Street in Mott Haven, Bronx. The Warehouse was home to many well-known local DJs, such as Bronx-born DJ Andre Collins, and balls hosted by LGBTQ activist Kevin Omni. "We really extended ourselves as family. The Warehouse not only gave us the music, the crowd and the dancing—it gave us a feeling," Omni described (Thomas 2017). The smell of the Warehouse was distinct as well—sage and incense because Collins would burn them at the start of each night (Dominus 2010). Omni reflected on one of the largest nights at the Warehouse, when Lil' Kim performed:

> There had to be over 2,000 people in there that night because she was very popular at the time. I got a chance to sit with her backstage before I brought her out. She said, "I love the gay kids." She was really interested in what I had to say, and I told her there were people there that night I hadn't seen for 15 years, because they were really sick. That night when I brought her out, they were screaming. (Thomas 2017)

Similar to Starlite in Brooklyn, the Warehouse was an institution that provided a setting for affirmation for Black gay people across the Bronx and beyond. The Warehouse was conceived by promoters Mike Stone of Studio

54 and Charles Jackson of Sound Factory Bar. Stone found a building owned by U-Haul; the moving equipment company was renting to Stone's acquaintances who were organizing straight functions. These functions—white college nights—were not well attended and in response Stone created the Warehouse. The first function that was held at the Warehouse was the Better Days Reunion on Memorial Day weekend in 1997 (Dominus 2010). As at the Starlite, Black LGBTQ people crowded the bar on the weekends. In 2006, the Warehouse closed after losing the lease of the building. Considering these two Black-owned clubs had closed, other bars started to incorporate designated hip-hop and house music nights into their event calendars, such as Boxers NYC located at 37 West Twentieth Street in Manhattan.

Remembering the Warehouse, in his thick New York accent, Milton exclaimed,

> The Warehouse was just everythang! I remember one night; it was Columbus Day [Indigenous People's Day] weekend. And I went to the Warehouse and the line was so long! Honey, I never seen a line so long, especially in this part of the Bronx. The promoter double-booked the club. There was college night attended mostly by white heterosexuals and Black gay night happening at the same time. There were two separate lines to get into the Warehouse. The Warehouse was massive enough to have multiple areas for everybody, though.

According to DJ Andre Collins, "There was something about the fact that it was an old warehouse and it had that nostalgic feeling. Sometimes rooms just have their own atmosphere. The main room was huge, with these high ceilings and wooden floor" (Dominus 2010). As Collins noted, rooms have their own atmosphere, and that atmosphere is created by what people do in the room—such as gettin' yo' life. Johnson (1998) describes the actions of Black gay men inside a nightclub in Washington, DC, who cry, kiss, shout, dance to the beat of the music, and wave their hands in the air, which is akin to Collins's statements about atmosphere and what people do in the room, gettin' yo' life. Therefore, the activities in the Warehouse, the predominantly Black gay nightclub in DC, and Langston's, as I observed, include repetitious practices that are unique to Black queer places, such as burning incense at the start of the night and singing to live music and house and hip-hop DJ sets, as well as passionately dancing with the same sex. These practices are world-making practices.

World-making is the means through which such spatial articulations are constituted. World-making is a practice that influences placemaking on a grander scale. Considering that hegemonic structures oppress and marginalize Black queer people, alternative systems are conceived that affirm Black queer people and their experiences. Alternative systems are conceived by Black queer people through disidentification (Muñoz 1999) to establish place that is devoid of the anticipation of commodification. Disidentification is a strategy that works on and against dominant ideologies and systems such as heteronormativity and commodification. Furthermore, Muñoz's (1999) disidentification transforms cultural logics from within to effect social transformation in support of Black queer people. Therefore, disidentification is a hermeneutic—which is a process of becoming, naming, and producing—that frames Black queer placemaking. Secondly, disidentification is a Black queer placemaking strategy whereby new social relations are envisioned by Black queer people. These new social relations are activated in Black queer places. These new social relations would be the blueprint for minoritarian counterpublic spheres across society (Muñoz's 1999).

Fiona Buckland's (2010) *Impossible Dance: Club Culture and Queer World-Making* discusses improvised dance—between two Black gay men, for example—as a primary strategy of queer world-making. Improvised dance in queer clubs, according to Buckland (2010), is a physical and embodied experience that places queerness at the center. Furthermore, Buckland (2010) associates queer world-making with Muñoz's (1999) "disidentification" and creative imagination for an alternative world for Black queer people:

> Queer lifeworlds embodied utopic imagination and power whereby queerness occupied the center, in which the heterosexual couple was no longer the referent or the privileged example of sexual culture. They existed within and drew some energy from not always oppositional relationships to the field of hegemonic power that attempted repeatedly and contingently to normalize hetero-orthodoxy. But only an impoverished, thing reading of these practices would deal lightly with the agency, meanings, and values participants drew from the pleasure of fitting in, as well as from resistance. Even in the dance club, at the end of the night when the music stopped and the lights came on, participants had to step back from the center stage of a queer lifeworld into a world that marginalized them. (Buckland, 2010, 33)

Here Buckland discusses values of queer lifeworlds, including power, imagination, and queerness. In addition, the creation of queer lifeworlds is the practice of laying claim to a site through physical and embodied practices that intentionally place queerness at the center during a particular time, particularly when the dance club closes.

Milton's sentiments regarding designated hip-hop or house music nights at predominantly white bars acknowledge the politics of consumption and its impact on community creation and Black queer world-making. The politics of consumption, according to Stuart Ewen (1984), must be understood as something more than what to buy, or even what to boycott. Black queer world-making is an act of resistance that challenges social codes that oppress Black queer people and narrow the possibilities of sexualities. Political theorist Jacques Attali (1985) discusses music composition as a foundation to influence improvised social dance in queer clubs, which, by extension, creates the possibilities of reimagination:

> We are all condemned to silence—unless we create our own relation with the world and try to tie other people into the meaning we thus create. This is what composing is. Doing solely for the sake of doing, without trying artificially to recreate the old codes in order to re-insert communication into them. Inventing new codes, inventing the message at the same time as the language. Playing for one's own pleasure, which alone can create the conditions for new communication. . . . It relates to the emergence of the free act, self-transcendence, pleasure in being instead of having. (134)

World-making is the authentic practice of centering queerness. By authentic, I mean the reliance on one's own desire, which supports being instead of having or consuming. Consumption is a social relationship, the dominant relationship that makes it difficult to create community in our society. For example, Boxers NYC is a gay bar in Chelsea, Manhattan. The bar is described as a sports bar that invites various sports teams and fans to meet. Boxers hosts bingo nights, karaoke, and drag viewing parties. However, the ways in which Black LGBTQ public culture is consumed by the Boxers NYC patrons and commodified under consumerism are rarely understood as authentic worlds for Black LGBTQ people. The designated hip-hop night one night a week at Boxers, for example, does not provide Black LGBTQ people with an intentional community of care that allows them to engage each other, make place, and represent Black LGBTQ public culture. These so-called hip-hop nights or house music nights are mechanisms of commodification and consumerism, considering the reliance on Spotify and Apple Music playlists rather than Black LGBTQ DJs. When political messages are commodified, it is easy for consumers to ignore them. And even though a product like rap articulates narratives of coming to critical political consciousness, it also exploits stereotypes and essentialist notions of Blackness (like ideas that Black people have natural rhythm and are more sexual) (hooks, 2014). Therefore, Black queer placemaking is a practice by Black LGBTQ people that aims to lay claim to place for Black LGBTQ public culture, communities of care, and people. These places are consequences of world-making imagined existing outside of communities of consumption. Again, world-making is about laying claim to place/s that allow Black queer people to exist in a space outside of the dominant space—particularly a space where the possibilities of sexualities and Black queerness are vast.

At Black Gay Pride in Brooklyn in the summer of 2018, I met Grayson. Grayson is a Black gay man in his midthirties who moved to New York in spring 2016. He currently lives in Crown Heights. He is a spatial epidemiology research coordinator in the Department of Population Health at New York University. He discussed the importance of world-making for Black queer people and their livelihoods. He described Langston's as a place that was necessary for Black queer people and their representation. Grayson was careful not to sensationalize Langston's but insisted that the pleasing experience of the bar outweighed its building aesthetics:

Langston's does have its "drawbacks," but one of the drawbacks . . . I think the drawback is that because how it is presented, it comes off as being I guess, quote unquote lower or a like trashy environment. But I think that's just because people are seeing the outside, and not for its pleasing experience and also not really understanding the underlying necessity of that experience regardless of what it looks like. I think it's important fundamentally for us to have a space for black and gay men or bisexual men to, you know, congregate and know kind of what you said, "Get your life." The white gays have Boxers and blah, blah, blah, hell, they have Industry and they have all of the Lower East Side pretty much. I'm like, what about us?

Here, Grayson suggests that world-making is a necessary strategy to create authentic Black queer places where Black queer people can authentically experience Black LGBTQ public culture. Therefore, the aesthetics of Langston's building are not as important as the community of care that is created within its walls because they are part of world-making.

Gettin' Yo' Life in Langston's

Langston's was a site of enmeshed encounters and interactions conditioned by the politics of race, class, gender, and sexuality. Langston's Brooklyn was located at 1073 Atlantic Avenue in Brooklyn, New York. The building was erected in 1930 on a 2,655-square-foot lot, and as noted previously, Langston's opened after 9/11, when many Black queer people in Brooklyn did not want to travel to Manhattan. The site not only provided a place for Black queer people across Brooklyn, but its presence in the landscape (built environment) marked—made public—Black LGBTQ public culture. J. B. Jackson (1995) discusses sense of place as a place's "influence." Specifically, Jackson (1995, 24) says, "our modern culture rejected the notion of a divine or supernatural presence, and in the eighteenth century the Latin phrase (*genius loci*) was usually translated as 'the genius of a place,' meaning its influence." Considering his notion, then, spatial sensations, events that are unique to Langston's, social encounters with people and objects, the forms of intervention that occur in the space, and the self-making that occurs within the space collectively render its influence—its sense of place.

According to Jamal Jordan (2019), and as I previously noted in the introduction, Langston's closed its doors permanently because Clark—an older Black gay man—accumulated over $70,000 in back rent, taxes, and expenses for city-mandated renovations. From March 2013 to October 2019, five building violations were issued to Clark, totaling $4,000 (Jordan 2019). The rising rent cost and building codes are symptoms of capitalism and urban structural powers. Langston's was one of only a handful of Black-owned LGBTQ clubs in Brooklyn as well as the state of New York. In an unsuccessful effort to save Langston's, Clark protested. He hung a large white banner from the top of the building: "Save Club Langston." On the opposite side of the street stood new residential buildings and commercial buildings, and concrete barricades and green fences surrounded construction sites.

World-making in the context of Black queer spatiality refutes narratives of inclusivity insofar as it eclipses Black queer spatial experiences of extraction. Inclusive senses of community for Black queer people are curated and maintained by Black queer people. Jackson (1995) argues that our cities have grown closer together, which has garnered a more inclusive sense of community, and that our habits, customs, and timetables are similar. Patricia Potts (2013) defines inclusion as an incessant process that aims to remove exclusionary pressures from various aspects of a society. She also notes that inclusion is concerned with increasing the capacity for whole people with intersecting, complex identities to be recognized, to be protected under the law, and to fully participate in their communities.

While most US cities have become denser than they were in the early 1990s, social geographies across most large cities have been characterized by anti-Black racism, socioeconomic deprivation, and spatial marginalization. Therefore, the political dimensions of space create a false sense of community[2] through the concerted or unintentional exclusion or extraction of Black people, particularly Black LGBTQ people, from housing opportunities and public space, generally by everyday people, brokers, developers, stakeholders, and landowners. A sense of community in Langston's was created through the clubgoers' distinctive activities, which produced sensorial experiences. The distinctive activities include gesturing, dancing—or "gettin' yo' life"—speaking, and naming.

Gestures

People of Color in Crisis focused on HIV/AIDS prevention for and by Black LGBTQ people across the city. It held community events in parks across Brooklyn, most of which took place in Fort Greene Park, located in Fort Greene, which was home to half of Brooklyn's Black population from 1870 to the early 2000s.[3] According to Milton, POCC held a number of events, such as the POCC Ball, and hosted parties at Pride in August throughout the 1990s and early 2000s. Milton said,

> You know we had the place packed! POCC knew how to throw a party. All the brothas from every borough would come out. But you know with any large group of Black people there may be haters. And there were! We made a way as best as we could due to the discrimination we experienced. I mean we had to do something! Who else but ourselves to help ourselves."

Milton then chuckled, snapped his fingers once, then shook his head.

Queer performance theorist Juana María Rodríguez (2014, 6) contends that gesturing "is a socially legible and highly codified form of kinetic communication, and . . . a cultural practice that is differentially manifested through particular forms of embodiment." Gesturing, then, is an alternative form of communication that is nonverbal. Following Kissine's (2013) discussion, speaking entails more than just using words; it also produces actions, or speech acts. In Black queer vernacular, speech is used to affirm, command,

2. The opportunity for Black and Black queer people to participate in democracy is cloaked in the sacrifice of Black leaders such as the late congressman John Lewis, who advocated for voting rights for Black Americans; Marsha "Pay It No Mind" Johnson, who advocated for gay liberation; and Alicia Garza, Patrisse Cullors, and Opal Tometi, who collectively founded the global Black Lives Matter movement that aims to dismantle systems of oppression that harm and expose Black people to premature death.

3. In the 1990s, Forte Greene, Brooklyn, was colloquially referred to as the Chocolate Chelsea (Lavers 2009).

supplicate, and promise. Considering these two forms of communication, when Milton snapped his fingers, it was a gesture to emphasize his statement that Black queer people had to look out for their community in the early 2000s.

Matt Richardson's (2013) *The Queer Limit of Black Memory: Black Lesbian Literature and Irresolution* explores Black queer lived experiences to discuss the ways in which vernacular involves queer ways of knowing that many Black dominant histories occlude, or do not acknowledge. Richardson (2013) uncovers rich Black queer histories and demonstrates the presence and influence of queerness in and on Black diasporic vernacular traditions. Richardson (2013) suggests that Black queer vernacular is a constant practice by Black queer people to represent their Black queer lived experience and discuss queerness as inherently Black. Marcus, who is a thirty-something-year-old Black man whose parents migrated from the Caribbean, reflected on Black queer places that once embodied Black queer vernacular in Brooklyn:

> There are also places that used to be spaces for queer Black folks in Brooklyn that are now gone. Bars like Starlite and clubs like The Lab and Club Saturn. The only available place left is Langston's and they don't offer price conscious parties.[4] Their liquor is more expensive than queer black friendly spaces in Brooklyn. They charge $15 to $20 at the door, and they don't take debit cards. It's very odd how antiquated they've remained. The music is good—it makes the kids want to dance though. It makes you wanna shake it. I typically hang out at Black-owned businesses. They include Brooklyn Moon, Ode to Babel, Beso, BKLYN Blend, Peaches, Cheryl's Global Soul, and one of my favorite Dominican joints, Salud. I also enjoy hanging out in Prospect Park and Herbert Von King Park.

As Marcus discussed the vanishing places where Black queer people could hang out, he clapped after the words "at the door." He clapped to emphasize the high entrance price at Langston's. His claps, in addition, are gestures that are unique to Black queer placemaking. Moreover, he refers to Langston's patrons as "the kids" not because they are actually kids, but in Black queer vernacular, "the kids" refers to Black queer people of all ages. Marcus refers to the dance forms that make the kids want to shake it. All things considered, Marcus suggests that Langston's—although pricey—is a Black queer world that is created for Black queer people to feel at home. Langston's, then,

---

4. At the time of this interview, Langston's was still open.

is imagined as a place where Black queer people can find fellowship, "hook up," and dance.

On another trip to Langston's on a late July night in 2018, I notice a line of ten Black men who are in their midtwenties to early forties. As I walk toward the back of the line, I notice there are at least four friend groups that make up the entrance line. As I stand in line, house beats pour out of the door each time the bouncer opens the door to allow for a few patrons to enter the dimly lit nightclub. After ten minutes, there are more people arriving at the club by foot as well as cab in groups of three and four.

The new arrivals dance to the end of the line. As I continue to wait, I notice that everyone seems to know one another. I overhear a man who appears to be in his early thirties snap his fingers and call out to another Black man who appears to be in his late twenties in the line. He yells, "Hey, stranger, long time!" To which the other gentleman replies, "I know, right! How you been, boo?" In addition to this exchange, as I near the entrance to the bar, I notice people who are standing in the line showing gestures of care—hugging and kissing one another on the cheek, followed by a smile and more "Hey, boo"s, and laughing with each other, snapping their fingers in the air as they pass one another in the growing line. Richardson (2013) refers to vernacular as a means to insert histories and lived experiences that are not discussed as a Black diasporic tradition. For example, drag is a vernacular performance that uses the body to *do* Black queerness. In addition, voguing is a type of vernacular performance, a dance form, that demonstrates Black queer epistemology using the body. The clubgoers' dance form is a bodily language that demonstrates Black queerness, while it is primarily a means to express oneself; it is a mechanism of Black queer placemaking, marking the site where the voguing occurs. For example, dance, such as voguing, is a product of Black LGBTQ public culture; it is regularly performed by Black queer people to insert histories and lived experiences in public.

Dancing—or "Gettin' Yo' Life"

Dancing—or "gettin' yo' life"—is a bodily act of expressing meaning using the body. Gettin' yo' life was demonstrated at the POCC Ball in 2008. Although I did not attend, I viewed recordings that were shared by one of my interlocutors. Gettin' yo' life is a dance form that is unique to the Black queer community that takes many forms, but it is an intense jaw-dropping dance form that gets many onlookers excited. In this case, dancers competed through voguing on a T-shaped stage in the park where the 2008 POCC Ball took place.

Two competitors pranced from the backstage to the center stage, their hips moving from left to right, to begin their dance routine. One of the competitors—a Black femme queen—was doing what is called a death drop, which is when a person spins and falls onto the floor back first. The competitor's wrists were bent, allowing their fingertips to balance their body. The competitor—a femme queen—pranced to the end of stage and spun and placed their hand on their hip, while their other arm stretched out at a 90-degree angle between their hip and their arm. According to my interlocutor, at another POCC event in 2004, gettin' yo' life happened on the main stage. The person who danced made their way from the backstage to the front stage, voguing to the beat of the music, supporting the creation of the Black queer world in a Brooklyn public park.

The creation of the Black queer world is conceived through a comprehensive system of distinctive activities by Black queer people that demonstrates spatial imagining. The spatial imagining is conceived by Milton and other event organizers. The spatial imagining is made real by the spatial configuration of the stage, the speakers, the music, and the ways in which Black queer people take place.

E. Patrick Johnson (1998) discusses dance in the Black gay community as both a sexual and a spiritual act; he draws direct connection between the "sacred" place of the church and the secular place of the nightclub. Johnson (1998, 413) says that the "sacred" place of the church, where the rhetorical discourse of the service censures and confines the body, is re-visioned within the secular space of the nightclub so as to liberate the body. The bodies on the dance floor are sexualized in their movements, as couples grope each other to the beat of the music, just as churchgoers move closer to the church pulpit, as arms, legs, and hands fling in sensual and provocative motion. The club space secularizes the whole notion of the "shout" or the "holy dance": a sexualized queer body in a club resembles a churchgoer's praise dance in a church of God. The result is that the dancer affirms both the sexual and the spiritual. Spatial imagining and alignment are acts that conceive of a space that encloses similar bodily expressions across various typologies and is nostalgic of a certain place.

Dancing was of course a prominent feature of the events I observed at Langston's as well, and in some cases the dancing started before patrons had entered the club itself. Consider another scene: I observe people waiting in line dancing to the music coming from inside the bar. Their hands are high in the air—similar to the ways that church goers express praise in a church setting—and the clubgoers' hips move from side to side as the music plays. As I make my way to the front of the line, the bouncer, a tall Black man well over six foot one who appears to be in his late fifties, asks me, "How you doin', brother?" I respond, "I'm good, and you?" as I simultaneously pull my ID out of my front pants pocket. Once he checks my ID, I turn around to take one last look at the entrance line. I notice a sea of Black men and three Black women in the line, all laughing and dancing in their smaller friend groups. This spatial experience—ranging from the music playlist to the familiarity with people in the bar—is adjacent to dominant spatial experiences. This experience reflects a Black queer sense of place, particularly the gestures, speech acts, dance, and imagining that take place inside the bar.

On the dance floor, there are Black men whose ages range from midtwenties to midthirties. Their bodies grind against one another to the beat of the music. The temperature of Langston's has to be above seventy degrees, as almost everyone on the dance floor has a napkin in one hand that is used to pat their face every so often. As I move through Langston's, I have to squeeze between sweaty bodies. Sweat runs down my back and I feel the other clubgoers' sweat on my arms. The feeling of the sweat against my arm is sensual. The feeling freezes time. I expect people to give me looks that did not approve of someone's sweat on them. However, I do not receive any negative looks. It is normal in this place. My sensorial experiences illustrate how Langston's is a space that is community focused and produced; it is a space where Blackness and queerness converge. I am at home; I feel like I can be myself, express myself through dance, gesture, or speech without anticipating violent backlash.

Speaking and Black Queer Vernacular

Borrowing from Kissine (2013) once again, speech acts may be used to affirm, command, supplicate, or promise, among other intentions. For example, speech acts in Black queer vernacular include these phrases, to name a few: "Oh chile!" "Kween!" and "Fierce!" As I have shown, Black queer vernacular uses words like "sis" and "queen" to mark a Black queer place—a safe Black queer world that has not yet been touched by the intentional commodification of Black queer public space. As Richardson (2013, 7) argues, Black queer vernacular or forms of expression "comment on and resist the oppression of queer sexualities and genders, as well as create queer kinship networks, communities, and alternatives to diasporic displacement." Here Richardson (2013) suggests that Black queer vernacular is a tool that dismantles oppressive structures and builds new systems that support Black queer people through its adoption and use. More specifically, when Black queer people speak to one another and use words like "sis" to refer to each other, they are making an intervention by resisting the adoption of normative language, which is limiting because its rules do not capture the full range and flexibility of Black LGBTQ culture. For example, normative language conflates gender and sex, which does not provide Black queer people with the tools to accurately describe their gender on their terms. Black queer people also engage in Black queer placemaking through spoken language, which is recognized once Black queer vernacular is heard.

During my interview with Milton, his statement about the spatial configuration of a POCC event included mention of a kinship tie—he referred to other Black queer people attending the 2004 POCC event, men in particular, as "brothas." Milton said:

> POCC always had a good turn out whether we were outside or in a club. We always had a place where Black LGBTQ people to gather and connect to each other. Our reach was far, and we always had to play some popular music and have people vogue to it. We had a good time making music fit into our culture so everyone can enjoy it. This is because we couldn't expect anyone else to do it for us, even make a space for us to be ourselves. All the work was our own, and our community appreciated it, and we knew we had to continue the work of making place for us.

Milton's comment suggests that Black LGBTQ people consistently care for one another because hegemonic structures do not support the multifaceted quotidian lives of Black LGBTQ people. Besides, normative systems fail to protect the lives of Black transgender women, to provide accessible and affordable health care to Black LGBTQ people, and to respond to the rising rates of Black LGBTQ homelessness across Brooklyn. Listening to Milton discuss care-work makes me feel protected, seen, and valued by the Black LGBTQ community.

At Langston's kinship connections are established when the bouncer refers to me as his "brotha." Of course, I am not biologically related to the bouncer, but he suggests some familiarity with me, which provides a sense of comfort before I step into Langston's. Furthermore, listening to the bouncer call me "brotha" makes me feel warm and calm. I recognize a sense of familiarity hearing "brotha" because it reminds me of Black spaces where Black people establish a connection with other Black people so as to remind each other, "I see you." Hearing "brotha" makes me feel appreciated as family in Langston's.

In addition, mutual recognition occurs when the bouncer establishes a kinship connection with me; I recognize the systemic value of kinship that makes Langston's as a product of Black queer world-making.

As I stand in the entrance line outside of Langton's, I hear other people refer to each other as "boo" as a term of endearment. I see people dance—moving their hips from side to side as "Control" plays inside the bar. Sometimes speech and gesture are combined, as when the people standing in line snap their fingers in the air, as if the expression is a way to say "yes" in agreement with others. This type of gesture is unique to Langston's and other Black queer worlds and places. As I stand in the line, I feel the bass line of the song underneath my feet. The black exit door opens every ten minutes as clubgoers exit the bar. "Control, now I've got a lot. Control, to get what I want!" the clubgoers sing in line, their heads moving from side to side to the beat of the music and their hands in the air. All of these actions are forms of Black queer placemaking, world-making, that mark Langston's as a Black queer place that is conceived or imagined by people attached to the site.

Naming

Naming is the act of labeling through language. The photographs of Black LGBTQ pioneers such as Langston Hughes affixed to each of the four walls in Langston's are a naming practice. Every time I enter Langston's, past the entrance fee counter, I notice to my right a framed photo of Hughes. I notice the face because I remember when I first researched Black artists in my public high school in Mobile, Alabama. When I notice the picture, I immediately feel Langston's is a home for me—or a place where the possibilities of identities are vast. The photographs reflect a sense of Black queer history.

On this particular evening, Dennis Ferrer's "Hey Hey" is blasting inside of Langston's. I can hear and feel the beat of the song as I walk through the entrance at 11:34 p.m. I give Nae, a forty-something-year-old Black woman, the $20 cover charge, and she barely makes eye contact with me, as there are so many patrons in line that she is in a hurry to get me through the entrance.

Once I charge through the black drape, I immediately notice three Black men and one Black woman on the dance floor directly in front of me dancing under the large silver disco ball—another element that marks or names the space as a nightclub space. The dance floor is in front of the foyer and in the center of the bar space. On the dance floor are butts swaying as people grind on each other. The Black woman is in her late twenties. She wears a denim dress, three bracelets around her right wrist, and platform leather boots trimmed in silver studs. She has on a wide-brimmed black hat over her blonde faux twists, which sway vigorously as she moves her body to the beat of "Hey Hey." The three Black men are next to each other and in front of their woman friend. Their bodies form a semicircle. The man to my right wears a pair of white shorts and a sky-blue tank top that shows his large chest tattoo of angel wings etched in his hazelnut skin. The man to my left wears denim shorts and a black, fitted V-neck T-shirt that pronounces the muscle definition in his arms and chest. The group appears to be in their early thirties. The neon lights shine blue, green, and red in every corner of the bar. Narrow streamers hang from the ceiling of the bar. As each neon light reflects on the streamers, a silver light flies against the silver disco ball that hangs one foot below ceiling, marking the center of the bar. All together, my experience of Langston's is textured by the way and the extent to which I interact with other people on the dance floor, Nae, the disco ball, and the bass line of Dennis Ferrer's song. Immediately, I feel the urge to express my true self because I understand the world-making that took place to provide me with the opportunity to express myself on my terms in a place where improvisational social dance is encouraged.

Upon further entering into the space, I walk past a clubgoer who says, "Yas! You betta do dat! Look at trade! He know he know me. C'mon, let's take a hoe stroll!" Neon lights—a curated light show to name the bar, again, a nightclub set for dancing—shine against the walls. Similar to the drape in the foyer, long black drapes cover the walls of the bar. DJ Smoove announces, "Come out to the floor and let loose, brother!" Someone from the dance floors yells to me. I walk over to the dance floor and I dance for the rest of the song under the silver disco ball. The smell of musk and masculine cologne fill the moist air. The cologne smells of cedar and vanilla. The smell reminds me of early Sunday mornings in Alabama where dew kisses blades of grass until the sun fully arrives. Sweat runs down the left side of my face, and I raise my hand to wipe it away. The bar's temperature causes me to raise my plastic cup and take a sip of my cocktail, which initially was more whiskey than Sprite, but is now water with a splash of Sprite. The bass from the speakers is so deep that I feel the floor vibrate. Unconsciously, my body starts moving to the beat. My head raises up and down to the beat of the song "Hey Hey." Once the song ends, the majority of the people on the dance floor make their way to the bar and the bathroom to wait for DJ Smoove to play the next song. Yet the beats and smells characteristic to Langston's are dimensions of the sensorial framework of Black queer spatiality. Once again, I feel at home, in a place where I belong, because the music sounds familiar to me, the vernacular I hear makes me feel like family, and the place smells like wood and cologne; it reminds me of Black-owned neighborhood bars I visited in the past.

The Downtown Landscape

The following week, I met Kenny, an older Black man who works in the health care industry. Kenny responded to my interview request through social media. I asked Kenny, "Have you been to Langston's before?"

He responded, "Yeah. Um . . . I'm just trying to think about the last time I been there, because it's been a couple of years. And prior to that last time, it was years since I been there. You know what I'm saying?"

I nodded my head in agreement and asked, "Can you can remember what is changing about Langston's and the surrounding area?" He responded,

> What's different . . . I want to say, they did some remodeling on the inside. [*Laughter*]. That's all I can think of right now. I know the crowd was a little different this time around. The crowd was a little bit younger than the crowd that was there before. Maybe it was the night I went. I don't know. I'm trying to think what else is different, and there is something different; I remember going there years ago, and I parked at something that appeared to be a parking lot across the street, and I parked there. Because that time I had a rental car. And I remember looking for parking, and I do recall looking there across the street and parking. Now, that parking lot is storage for construction that going on for the new high-rises. That right there is different. I can't think of anything else right now.

I asked Kenny, "So where do you hang out right now? Or do you hang out at the lounges?" He said,

> Yeah, I don't go out that often. Um . . . the last few times I did go out, it was in Brooklyn and it was the Happy Lounge [Happiness Lounge]. I don't know if you're familiar with it. It's on St. John, between Utica and Ralph. Or . . . Rochester? But anyway, I've been there the times I've been out. It's between that place and . . . Boxers in Manhattan a few months back. It was okay. It's definitely not my place to hang out.

I responded, "Why isn't it your place to hang out?" He said,

I was there because some of my coworkers from my job wanted to go. And it's like right there next to my job. I think we went a couple of hours after work. We hung out in the neighborhood a little bit and went there because it was convenient. But it's definitely not one of my hang-out spots. I'm trying to be as honest as possible. [*Laughter*]. No, because this is good for me, too. I mean, the very first time I went there I was like, I don't know. The very first time I went there, someone brought me there as well. There was a lot of white boys there, and I don't know. I don't know, I just don't hang out at places where there's whole lot of white guys. See that was one of the things that stood out for me. Not that I have an issue with um, you know, white people. It's just something I'm not used to. Normally, when I would often go out, it was either Black or Latino clubs. I think that has a lot to do with music selections, too. You know what I mean? You go into a white establishment, and music is a large part of going out. If you want to go out and have a good time, you want to hear great music. If I'm in a white club, and they are playing shit I can't relate to, I can't relate to it. I mean, that's one of the main things.

I nodded and said, "Okay, they're playing Taylor Swift, and not Big Freedia?"

Kenny responded with excitement, "Right! That's one of the main reasons why I can't relate to white clubs. Or Boxers. I don't go there that often, but what I remember is that they are open most days of the week, and I think the nights where I think people go are Friday and Saturday. And I think they have what's called a Black night, you know what I'm saying?"

I responded, "Yes, that's a common thing—having a gay night or a hip-hop night. Is there a cover at Boxers?"

Kenny quickly responded, "Nope, I don't remember paying to get in."

I continued, "So, like, talk about the last you went there: What was the crowd like? Older or younger? Are people dancing, or is it more of a lounge?" Kenny said,

It was definitely crowded. I didn't see anybody dancing. They have a couple of pool tables in the back. They have this back area where you can go outside and smoke. There's two levels. The first is where they have the bathroom, coat check, and video games. Old school video games. There's a lounge area to the left when you walk into the bar. So, you can congregate in that area. There's chairs and shit in that area. People are in there lounging. Then there's a bar, there's two bars. No one is dancing. That's an interesting assessment. I never realized. No one is dancing. What kind of difference that could make. As for the demographics, um, I was saying before, there's mostly white people there more than anything, like I was saying before. Um, you have Black people, Latinos, ciswomen. Um, I'm trying to think about the age demographic. I want to say like for the most part for people in their thirties and forties. At least that's how they look. They have, like, a couple of locations in Manhattan. They got one in Chelsea, and one in Hell's Kitchen. I think.

I nodded at Kenny and asked him, "Do you feel empowered in Boxers as a Black gay man?" He laughed and responded,

I definitely didn't feel empowered, because I felt out of place. You know what I mean? I felt out of place, and the weird thing about it is, I went there about three different times. Um, but each time I went, I went with somebody; it was their suggestion. I felt out of place. I was telling you why before. In terms of power or feeling empowered, or power—I don't know if I felt powerless in Boxers but I will say that, I'm trying to make the connection between feeling uncomfortable and I really don't fit in. I'm trying to connect that to power. I think for anybody, if they don't feel uncomfortable, that it does something with your ability to feel empowered. I'm just trying to make that connection. I definitely felt less empowered because it was an environment that I just wasn't used to. You know what I mean? Whenever I go out, and when I started going to Boxers, it had been a long time since I had been out to a club, and my friend wanted me. I was coming from somewhere, and I ran into a friend that I hadn't seen in years.

I thanked Kenny and prompted, "Now, say I was shooting a movie, and I just walked up to you, and I was like, you know, tell me about gentrifying Brooklyn in five seconds."
He laughed and said, "In five seconds though?"
I said, "Yeah, tell me what you would want them to know in your perspective." Kenny responded,

Okay, I would want them to know that the only good thing about gentrification is that some neighborhoods will become diversified. That's the only good thing about it. But there's also some disadvantages. I'll give you an example. There's a store on my block that I would frequent; whenever I needed something I would go in there and chill with them, I got to know them. Like hard. I got to know two of the guys who work there. You know what I'm saying, I would crack jokes with them and all that type of stuff. You know what I'm saying? Umm, two . . . for the first two years I lived in this neighborhood it was quiet, then shortly after two years, they started doing construction inside the store. I was happy for them. It was cramped, and I thought they were getting more room; they were going to get more products in there. I thought the construction would make it more convenient for the people who came there. The next thing I know they close the whole store. Then, I was like oh shit, they're about to turn this into something big for us. So, when they reopened it, the whole shit just looked different, they had glass doors, and it was just all different . . . so I go inside. I'm looking, and the menu is new, everything is new. They got all this organic shit, and I was like *okay*! I mean I like that, but I was also looking for the things I would buy when I would go in there. I'm not against organic food. You know what I'm saying. But I was so used to buying things I would usually get in there. Where is this, where is that. Then, I looked at the menu, and I'm thinking they have all this shit here. Then I started thinking gentrification, right. Then, I noticed this guy walk into the store and he was like oh shit, everything look mad different. He was like gentrification renovation. I thought that was kind of funny when he put that phrase together. They put this high-rise up across the street. It just went up maybe six months prior to the renovation. Then they did the renovation, and it turned into a whole completely different store. The whole ambience is different. I don't even go in there anymore. They don't have shit that I want. Then they jacked up the prices. So, for me, that sums it up for me right there. For Brooklyn, that's gentrification for me. I don't even go there anymore. You know what I'm saying? You attracting all these white people, but when you was building your foundation from the bottom up, it was us. You know what I'm saying? Who were your customers? Now you just flipped it on us . . . Sorry, I was a little excited about sharing that story.

I started to finish up the interview. "Thank you for those details, Kenny. I appreciate you for sharing your perspective. I now want to know what gentrification is like in Brooklyn, and how it is impacting you." Kenny said with excitement,

That's exactly what is it. I'm all for diversifying communities, but not at our expense. You know what I'm saying? I was watching stuff on gentrification a couple of months back. There were some videos I was browsing on You-Tube related to gentrification and I was watching them, and it led me to a whole bunch of other stuff. They were talking about the Whole Foods they put on 125th Street, and not only that but a lot of other establishments up in Harlem. You know, the type of impact that it has on poor people that live on there. You know what I'm saying? Because there's still a lot of . . . it's still Harlem. You still have people who are struggling. Then, you have these property managers who are buying up property, and it's driving up property values, and it's forcing people to move out. You know what I mean? So, back to my point, having diversity is great. But you're pushing people out of neighborhoods. Pushing people out of Harlem, Brooklyn, then where we going, Bronx? Or Queens?

I thanked Kenny for his time and sharing his experience with me and we parted ways.

During my field observations, Langston's sat across from a massive development project illuminated by many light poles and surrounded by a tall green fence. Langston's, however, was lit only by the exterior lamps, distant light poles, and traffic headlights. There was a stark difference between the two sides of the street.

People waiting outside of Langston's in the summer of 2018 stood in the foreground of the luxury high-rise residences and busy street and pedestrian traffic on Atlantic Avenue. This dichotomy of social activities—one more dramatic in scale than the other—reflects the symptoms of a critical juncture in the geography of capitalism, one that highlights the nexus between capitalism and culture. Capitalism, according to David F. Ruccio (2014), designates an economic structure that operates as a system. As a system, it is a mode of production that includes inherent conflicts, contradictions, and subjectivities that subsequently reproduce capitalism and take control of the environment. Ruccio (2014, 38–39) writes, "Both the initial emergence and the subsequent reproduction of capitalism, if and when they occur, often lead to social dislocations and acute crises; they are also conditioned by the most carried cultures and social identities."

Nigel Thrift (2002) posits that total control of land is not possible amid a new industrial revolution that is predicated on making people—inhabitants of environments—as well as environments more productive. To take this point a step further, a by-product of the second industrial revolution is the making of certain visible, digestible cultures in the landscape—the built environment. This by-product is certainly congruent with the commodities in the landscape—land and high-rise condo. Interestingly, Thrift (2002) highlights three characteristics of the ways in which the built environment near Langston's can be conceived in the political moment, namely, the second industrial revolution: the cultivation of identity, inhabitation, and memory.

Consider the ways in which queer spaces have been squeezed out of the public sphere through legislation, hyper-policing, and self-appointed neighborhood watchmen. This consideration is part and parcel to interplace competition. Frankly, Times Square was at one point a red-light district, but capitalism, which is inherently competitive, changed it to one of the most quintessential capitalist sites in the world. Now, my point here is this: spatial change has social consequences—crises—that Marxist geographies capture and analyze. The social consequences demonstrated in *Times Square Red, Times Square Blue* (Delany 1999), for instance, reify the construction of places through spatial practices. Using a postmodern lens, the place that Times Square became after gentrification is the material edifice of memories rooted in white supremacy, colonization, and antiqueer and anti-transgender paranoia. Take, for instance, the ways in which neighborhood branding has been a spatial trend since the mid-1990s. There are neighborhoods like the Castro (San Francisco), Hillcrest (San Diego), Dupont Circle (Washington, DC), Boystown (Chicago), Melrose (Phoenix, Arizona), and a plethora of others for a reason. Primarily, the cultural politics of capital accumulation and place construction are founded on themes or social crises related to capitalism—appropriation, commodification, and domination. This is not to confuse queer placemaking with social movements led by people or struggles for socially just reinvestment, but to underscore the ways in which capitalism has been *the* socioeconomic force in reshaping the landscape through the logic of capitalist development, which renders uneven development as such capitalism continues to thrive, dominate, and control places and dwellings and their inhabitants.

Postmodern theorist David Harvey (1992, 599) writes that "the characteristic response of the welfare state capitalism has been either to place such marginal groups under tight surveillance or, at best, to induce a condition of dependency in which state support provides justification to 'suspend all basic rights to privacy, respect, and individual choice.'" Therefore, the luxury residences that pepper the Brooklyn landscape (built environment) are a commercialized area filled with big box stores that reflect a consumerism culture in Brooklyn that increases the likelihood that Black LGBTQ people are surveilled. This is to say that regardless of what can be represented as a certain space, what lies at the heart of its conception is capital accumulation. All this considered, Thrift (2002) characterizes a so-called second industrial revolution as if any industrial revolution sits outside of the reach of capitalism. Unfortunately, it does not. Then, perhaps, Thrift (2002) may see the ways in which social control is a by-product of capitalism and, by extension, this socalled second industrial revolution in which places are constructed.

As a place, Langston's provided a stage for Black queer people to conceive, perceive, enact, and facilitate their social and political agencies. Margaret Farrar (2011, 727) posits that places "provide a grounding (quite literally) for the enactment of 'we, the people.'" Farrar (2011, 725) explores the intersection of place, space, landscape, and memory by acknowledging that the co-constitutive qualities of place and identity are predicated on memory because all events happen at a particular time and space along the space-time continuum. As a result, memory, identity, and place become entangled; that is, one quality cannot be fully sensed or recognized without acknowledging or interpreting an image and imageability through one or two alternative quality/ies. For example, I cannot recount any memory of Langston's without acknowledging where I was located at a particular point in time inside Langston's. I recall the dominating temperature inside of Langston's, the sweat that rolled down the necks of the clubgoers, the bright neon-green lights, and the large silver disco ball in the center of the dance floor by remembering where I was located when those things happened in front of my eyes. Therefore, when I remember Langston's, my interpretation of the event and place is filtered through my experience as a Black queer cisgender man, and by extension, informs worlding. Place, space, landscape, and memory are not mutually exclusive, but they are interdependent. As Farrar (2011, 725) argues, "Places become written on the body, wired into memory; places become part of us, quite literally. Through place-making, we reify both our individual and collective identities. To paraphrase Connolly here, when political theorists ignore this *spatial* register of being, we risk not fully comprehending how embodied memory functions in our lives and in our political imagination."

Following her theorization of place, memory becomes a critical dimension of place as it intersects or is remembered with a personal and collective memory associated with that place, which again is experienced and interpreted through my identity formation. I would be remiss if I did not acknowledge that a placeless memory is nostalgia, which is the default response; it is the acute form of place memory. The cologne that reminded me of my hometown Mobile, Alabama, reminded me of the people and their histories. I was reminded of my own history in Langston's; I experienced nostalgia for a certain place and time. Farrar (2009, 728) concludes that nostalgia is an action in which a memory is consciously relived through the body in present time; nostalgia is also prompted by a sensation, such as a smell. Have you ever smelled a distinct odor that reminds you of a certain event at a certain place and time? This experience is nostalgia. To employ Black queer spatiality is to experience nostalgia. When we experience nostalgia—a longing for a particular place and time—it is a bodily experience, often prompted by sensory data (a particular smell or taste) and producing physical effects (depression, illness). Nostalgia allows us to be "thrust back, transported, into the place we recall" (Casey 2000, 201). And accounts of people's experiences of displacement—whether as migrants, exiles, or refugees—repeatedly emphasize the interconnections between body, mind, and place.

Conclusion

This chapter has focused on the sociopolitical and material effects of gentrification and displacement on the significance of Langston's using world-making as a means to discuss the sensuous geographies of Langston's. I argued that Black queer placemaking involves Black queer gestures, including snapping of fingers, Black queer vernacular, homoerotic dance forms, and spatial imaginings. Black queer spaces are produced by the racial, gender, and sexual politics that are embedded in place-specific and strategic modes of contestation and resistance. While I established a working image and example of Black queer sense of place, I discussed histories of anti-Blackness, homophobia, economic deprivation, and spatial segregation that necessitate Black queer senses of place as they continue to be constantly under threat. Black queer spatiality requires a sociohistorical analysis of Black queer extraction. Our Black queer worlds—such as Langston's—are spatial possibilities made by people, which also remove barriers that disallow, threaten, and destabilize systems that support Black queer spatiality.

Although Langston's Brooklyn was forced to close, Black queer community formations will always emerge elsewhere. Black queer people have learned the meaning of resiliency from their life experience. They have had to recover from a slate of US social issues, including racism, sexism, homophobia, transphobia, police brutality, housing inequity and displacement, transportation inequality, exclusion, institutional mistrust, and lack of representation. Black queer people, moreover, have witnessed marked Black queer sites close, historically. Many sites, including Langston's Brooklyn, Happiness Lounge, and Starlite, are defunct. Black queer spaces are often under constant threat of erasure by the state; they are fragile. Black queer spatial fragility is a by-product of systemic oppressions, including racial capitalism. Yet Black queer people challenge racial and sociospatial injustice, and by extension, extraction and policing of Black queer people's bodies and their produced marked spaces from most gentrifying areas.

Racial capitalism is a transnational modern world system that advances colonization. Racial capitalism and colonization rely upon slavery, imperialism, and genocide. Cedric J. Robinson's *Black Marxism* explains the racial component of capitalism and its phenomenological themes by discussing the racialism that characterized Western feudal society and highlighting the impact of the racial order on the organization of labor under capitalism. Robinson (2020) clarifies that racism does not simply distinguish people based on whether they are European or not; racism also impacted the internal relations of Europeans, ideologically and in actuality. Robinson (2020, 2) defines racialism as "the legitimation and corroboration of social organization as natural by reference to the racial components of its elements." As a material force, racialism under capitalism conditions the development, organization, and growth of traditional capitalist social structures. Robinson (2020, 2) uses the term "racial capitalism" to signify the relationship between racialism and capitalist social structures. Robinson's (2020) racial capitalism explains the limitations of Karl Marx and Friedrich Engel's theories of social revolution:

> The Negro—whose precedents could be found in the racial fabrications concealing the Slavs, the Irish and others—substantially eradicated in Western historical consciousness the necessity of remembering the significance of Nubia for Egypt's formation, of Egypt in the development of Greek civilization, of Africa for imperial Rome, and more pointedly of Islam's influence on Europe's economic, political, and intellectual history. From such a creature not even the suspicion of tradition needed to be entertained. In its stead there was the Black slave, a consequence masqueraded as an anthropology and a history. The creation of the Negro was obviously at the cost of immense expenditures of psychic and intellectual energies in the West. The exercise was obligatory. It was an effort commensurate with the importance Black labor power possessed for the world economy sculpted and dominated by the ruling and mercantile classes of western Europe. (4)

Racial capitalism is shaped by perversions and contradictions that are characteristic of its primary social system, capitalism, and its surrogate—the state. By perversions and contradictions, I am referring to the interdependence of racial capitalism and the state to chart normative prescriptions of race, gender, sexuality, and place while committing and concealing racial violence against Black people and people of color. Racial capitalism and the state arrange social structures and relations that are sited in the means of social reproduction. The subsequent arrangement is often devoid of racial equity and theories of justice, including queer approaches to justice. To include racial equity and justice in the social structure would mean that ideally the system would provide protection and other forms of support to people who have historically not been in proximity to power. Showing resiliency, Black queer people constantly challenge traditional social structures through protest, performance, and placemaking to affirm their own personhood.

CHAPTER 3

Care-Work, Performance, and Kinship Labor in Happiness Lounge

In February 2019, I received an Instagram direct message from Montae. Montae is a self-aware and extremely extroverted Black gay man in his midthirties. He is slender in stature, stands five feet eleven, and is a direct and intentional communicator. In 2018 he lived in a 1940s-era apartment building in Prospect Lefferts Gardens, a residential neighborhood east of Prospect Park. There is a level of housing diversity in Prospect Lefferts Gardens, with increasingly expensive housing options. As I stand on Fenimore Street, I notice a large brick apartment building standing next to a multistory single-family home. Lush trees line the sidewalk and several cars are parked on the street. Brownstone apartments fill the west side of the street. Each brownstone has its own entrance gate and fencing. Trees that line the street have barriers around their bases. Also, several cars are parked on the street. As of March 2021, Montae has moved out of Brooklyn due to the lack of building maintenance in the apartment building and its high rental cost.

"I don't live in Brooklyn anymore," Montae said.

Like I kept having problems with the ceiling, the slow elevator, there were bugs all up in the apartment, and maintenance was slow to get anything done! And they didn't lower my rent! Like . . . what? The apartment is an older building so of course things will break. When things break, fix it. I pay to live in a maintained building. They were not maintaining the building.

I thought for a minute. If you not gonna maintain my apartment and the building where I live, then why I am here? I moved to Harlem.

Montae's comment suggests that his Brooklyn apartment is not livable considering that the management company does not complete maintenance requests. As a result of the lack of building maintenance, Montae decided to moved out of the borough of Brooklyn to rent an apartment in Harlem. Similarly, Langston's was forced to close because its owner, Calvin Clark, did not complete city-mandated renovations to the building and pay back rent.

In the previous chapter, I discussed Black LGBTQ bars and clubs that have closed and how Black queer people engage in Black queer placemaking practices to resist their spatial marginalization and produce alternative, affirming sites. I also argued that Black queer people engage in distinct activities to make place. In this chapter, I discuss care-work, kinship labor, and performance as practices that are unique to Black queer placemaking. Black queer placemaking, as I have defined it in chapter 2, is a practice that aims to manifest Black queer worlds. Black queer worlds are those that have yet to be touched by systems of commodification. Commodification refers to the system of exchange between people and institutions. Commodity production erases subjectivity and agency. Roderick Ferguson (2004, 7) cites Marx in his explanation of commodification: "Marx states that commodification produces people as mentally and physically dehumanized beings." Thus, there is room for understanding that Black queer worlds are conceived without anticipation of economic gain.

In this chapter, I argue that Happiness Lounge is a community of care with a Black queer sense of place where Black LGBTQ people perform care-work and kinship labor and engage in performance that places queerness at the center. I provide three examples of care-work, kinship labor, and performance unique to Happiness Lounge. I discuss care-work in Happiness Lounge by focusing on the events that are organized there. Kinship labor is about building connections with people, for example through language. I explore performance labor by discussing a patron's solo vocal performance.

Heteronormativity recognizes kinship structures as groups of people who share similar origins, affiliations, and genetics, while Black LBGTQ communities such as Ballroom communities forge new familial structures. Marlon M. Bailey (2014) discusses kinship and gender systems in Ballroom culture in Detroit, Michigan:

The gender system defines the roles that members serve in the house. In Ballroom culture, houses are kinship structures that are configured socially rather than biologically. Although houses are mostly social configurations, at times, they serve as literal homes or gathering places for their members (Arnold and Bailey 2009). These mostly social configurations are typically named after *haute couture* designers, but some are named after mottos and symbols that express qualities and aims with which the leaders want a house to be associated. These alternative families, as it were, are led by "mothers" and "fathers," house parents who provide guidance for their "children" of various ages, race and ethnic groups (usually Black and Latino/as), and genders and sexualities, who come from cities and regions throughout North America. (493)

Here Bailey (2014) discusses kinship as a social connection to other people, and the actual work of making those connections and their maintenance is kinship labor. The actual work—kinship labor—is represented in Black queer histories and politics.

Black queer histories and politics serve as critical sites "providing new ways of contesting traditional family and kinship structures—of reorganizing national and transnational communities based not on origin, filiation, and genetics but on destination, affiliation, and assumption of a common set of social practices or political commitments" (Eng et al., 2005, 7). In addition, I explore atmosphere, nostalgia, and sensation in Happiness Lounge to clarify its Black queer sense of place. All things considered, the symbols and meanings across Happiness Lounge indicate a Black queer sense of place by its atmosphere, sensations, and nostalgia, and notably, performance, kinship labor, and care-work in Happiness Lounge underscore the geographic bent to race, gender, and sexuality. In other words, I will index Happiness Lounge's looks, feels, smells, and sounds.

I describe a Black queer sense of place by applying Black queer spatiality to Happiness Lounge. First, I introduce Happiness Lounge. Then, I explain a Black queer sense of place by indexing the sensuous geographies, atmosphere, and nostalgia in Happiness Lounge. I explore how racialized queer gender moves through space and the mechanisms that Black queer people adopt to create meaningful places. In particular, I highlight the aspects of the Happiness Lounge that affect patrons by exploring the senses and their relationship to place. Finally, I offer demonstrative themes that summarize the representational and nonrepresentational spatial articulations that are fundamental to a Black queer sense of place, including care-work, performance, and kinship labor. Performance labor is the actual work or strategies that people do; the "labor" in performance labor signifies the means by which people exert energy to make a statement with their body. José Muñoz (1999) relies on queer performances—which are inherently political—to conceive, forge, and execute survival strategies such as disidentification: "Disidentification is meant to be descriptive of the survival strategies the minority subject practices in order to negotiate a phobic majoritarian public sphere that continuously elides or punishes the existence of subjects who do not conform to the phantasm of normative citizenship" (Muñoz 1999, 4). Kinship labor is a type of labor that includes the actions that people participate in to forge familial connections to other people. Care-work consists of the intentional actions of supporting people and oneself through various means. Care-work, moreover, is social reproduction, or how we live (see Coe 2011; Lawson 2007; Aranda 2003).

I learned about Happiness Lounge after the closing of Club Langston. The space where Langston's used to be now has large, black garage doors covering the entrance. The garage doors are locked with two silver padlocks. Above the garage doors is a banner that reads "Wu Lounge Coming Soon Formerly Known as Club Langston's." The letters "Wu Lounge" are printed in the colors of the traditional gay pride flag—red, orange, yellow, green, blue, and purple. Below the written text is a graphic: silhouettes of hands carrying the traditional gay pride flag, which indicates the type of business that is taking the place of Langston's, specifically a bar that recognizes the traditional gay flag, rather than the updated flag, which incorporates additional colors representing Black, Brown, and Indigenous peoples. This is a sobering outcome for the beloved Black queer space of Langston's Lounge.

On September 5, 2019, the *New York Times*'s "Endangered Spaces" section featured Calvin Clark and his fundraiser campaign, with its $70,000 goal (Jordan 2019). The article, written by Jamal Jordan, explained that Clark stood outside of Langston's for twelve hours a day for ten days in February to raise awareness of the fundraising campaign to cover the expenses for Langston's, including back rent totaling over $70,000 and city-mandated renovations, including new walls, new bathrooms, and new floors. Clark also added new sound systems to the list of renovations. Clark said, "I did everything I could do to take a stand. But in the end, it wasn't enough" (Dominus 2010). Although Clark's fundraising goal was $70,000, he made approximately $18,000. As a result, Langston's closed and Wu Lounge (see figure 3.1) opened in its place.

Thomas Beauford, who grew up on Franklin Avenue in Brooklyn, was quoted in the article on the closing of Langston's: "There's definitely a void in the neighborhood now." After reading this, I called Frank—an older Black man who lives in Brooklyn and plays a prominent role in the Ballroom scene—hoping that he could identify an alternative to Langston's; in other words, Where might Black LGBTQ people go now that Langston's is closed? Without hesitation, Frank said, "You have to check out Happiness Lounge. We in there. We don't have Langston's now so more community events might happen there." The "we" in Frank's statement is intentional. He means Black

FIGURE 3.1. Wu Lounge. Photograph by the author.

LGBTQ people across Brooklyn will begin to choose Happiness Lounge as a safe space for now.

To the right of Happiness Lounge is a Caribbean restaurant named Tasty Bites. To the left of the lounge is VP Universal Salon, a comprehensive salon where many locals go to get box braids, a haircut, or a pedicure. The signage on the facade of Happiness Lounge is white and burgundy. The top of the signage has a white background, and the numbers 1458 are printed in burgundy; a burgundy graphic of a cocktail cup is printed on the far left side of the sign. The words "Happiness Lounge" are printed in black across the top of the sign. A burgundy-colored strip stretches across the bottom of the sign. In the foreground of the strip is the name "Happiness Lounge Inc." Blue and red neon signs rest in the front window. The blue neon sign, which is on the left, reads "Bud Light," and the red neon sign, which is on the right reads, "Budweiser."

"You Have to Be Open for Something New"

I step off of the number two train at Crown Heights–Utica Avenue and make my way toward the stairs, about twenty feet away. I walk past an older Black gentleman in a black wheelchair. Before I can put one foot on the first step to ascend, I notice a Black woman in her early forties with a young child in tow. I stop at the bottom of the stairs and move slightly to the right to allow them to safely walk to the subway. "C'mon, you got it. You can walk," the woman says. The young child is carefully walking down the steps, each foot landing on each step. After his fourth step, the woman picks him up by his left arm to help him jump to the next step. "Thank you, baby," the woman whispers to me as they pass by. The spatial dimensions of the lived experience of race and gender and the lived experience of space includes both racial and gender dimensions. Summers (2019) discusses spatial realities of race in Washington, DC. She argues that the racialization of space brings into focus the identification of racial minorities and their subsequent stereotypes. Summers (2019, 13) contends, "To spatialize race speaks to the production of social relations, institutions, representations, and practices in space within the context of race. The racialization of space is the organizing principle through which unequal and uneven development takes place, rather than the results of this development." Here Summers (2019) discusses the inherent racialization of space by engaging people, institutions, and intentional actions in public. Once space becomes racialized, space is ripe with meanings that people consume and make sense of, which informs development efforts. Taking her point further, my interaction with the Black woman and the young Black boy demonstrates that race and gender are co-constitutive dimensions of the lived experience of space. For example, when I notice a Black woman and child walking down the stairs to the subway platform, gender and race are meanings attached to the space. When I hear the Black woman telling the child, "C'mon, you got it. You can walk," I immediately become aware of the care-work the woman is engaged in. At this moment, I move to the side to support the Black woman's care-work by allowing the small child and the woman to make their way down the stairs without my body disrupting the small child's walking path. Once they reached the bottom of the stairs, the Black woman acknowledged my small but significant pause in support of her care-work effort by saying, "Thank you, baby." When she said this, I felt a warm feeling from the gentle response that creates a positive connection between the two of us in the subway station.

When I emerge from the Crown Heights–Utica station and begin walking toward Happiness Lounge, it is a very dark night. Only the headlights from passing cars light the green street signs. The smell of Caribbean food permeates the night air and loud bass from a passing car pierces the air; the narrow sidewalk even shakes beneath my feet. After the car passes, I notice two Black men in their thirties arguing with each other on the other side of the street from me. One of the men says, "Nawl, I need you to tell me the truth, now!" Then the other man responds, "Whatchu mean? I did, bae!" I continue walking north toward Happiness Lounge; I reflect on a recent conversation about the Black queer experience in gentrifying Brooklyn. According to Summers (2019, 15), "gentrification is understood as involving the displacement of lower-income Blacks and other people of color with white newcomers who possess higher incomes. Despite multiple definitions of gentrification, most scholars and the general public can abstractly account for feelings of neighborhood change." Marcus calls me to have a conversation as I stand outside of Happiness Lounge. I ask Marcus if he can talk about his relationship to Brooklyn, and he is excited to share his story with me:

> I was born and raised in Bedford Stuyvesant, Brooklyn. My parents both emigrated from the Dominican Republic. I'm of Dominican and Haitian descent. I feel very fortunate to have grown up in Brooklyn, but also to get to experience it both from the eyes of immigrants and from my experience as a first-generation American. I grew up in abject poverty, living in public housing. I am fortunate to have experienced poverty and to have lived in the projects in Brooklyn. Growing up, there was a high concentration of non-profit organizations servicing the poor, churches that expended services to us, and also a sense of community even during the crime wave of the early

to mid-'90s. None of this has remained. I'm not nostalgic about that time, but I now see how poor, low-income, and working-class folks who are in desperate need of services have to leave their neighborhood, and sometimes their borough, to access those services. I also want you to know that I want to return to the idealism I had in my youth about Brooklyn. My body is relieved at that time. I enter Black queer social spaces in Brooklyn knowing that more people will have my back, that there is allyship present, and that I can be unapologetically a queer, Afro-Latino. That's not something I could own before.

As a housing advocate, Marcus shares with me that Brooklyn's cultural and social landscape is changing as well. He adds,

> As a whole, the cultural and social landscape of Brooklyn is changing. Neighborhoods are not only gentrifying but are also becoming denser, which is evident through the constant scaffolding you see on blocks throughout Brooklyn. The quality of life for residents in gentrifying and gentrified neighborhoods is getting better. Crime is going down. As an example, East New York—a neighborhood once characterized by its high rate of crime—has not had any murders since December 2018. This is emblematic of what's happening to high-crime neighborhoods throughout the borough, including Brownsville/Ocean Hill, East New York, Canarsie, and Flatbush. We're also seeing an increase in affordable housing for poor, low-income, and middle-class families. The political economy of Brooklyn is also changing as pockets of the boroughs—neighborhoods like Williamsburg, Dumbo, and Brooklyn Heights—are becoming hubs for tech, media, and workspace companies. We're seeing the consistent deregulation of rent-stabilized apartments, more civic engagement and participation from our neighbors, and more greens-paces. I don't sense the same familial community that I grew up with in the '90s, because the violence of gentrification has characterized everyone's sense of community and belonging. Churches are being converted into condos, bodegas to coffee shops, storefronts to boutiques and restaurants. Entire classes of people are being targeted because of a subscription to capitalists' tropes.

Continuing the conversation, I ask Marcus about pockets of Brooklyn that have become safety nets for Black queer people. Without hesitation, he says,

> Neighborhoods such as Bedford Stuyvesant, Crown Heights, Ditmas Park, Clinton Hill/Fort Greene—have become safety nets for queer Black folks

to live in. We are moving there in droves, something that is evident to me by the number of queer and trans folks I see in social spaces. What's more special is that we're also living in communal spaces, where we are intentionally cohousing and deliberately building community where we live. What this looks like to me is hosting social gatherings together, cooking with one another, communing together. Brooklyn is gentrifying and with it is the meaning of "safe space." What's happening in an already gentrified Brooklyn to queer Black folks is an example of what's happening throughout this country. As we progress, we assimilate. I think the question we have to pose isn't what's being dismissed or denied from our queer bodied experience, but would we rather have queer Black social spaces, or safe social spaces that are integrated and inclusive?

These pockets of Brooklyn—according to Marcus—suggest a preferable space; these pockets support Black queer mobility and well-being. On the one hand, Marcus recognizes the ways in which Black people are impacted by gentrification when he says that Black queer people are building community where we live. On the other hand, the two men who were arguing on the sidewalk while we were talking indicate the Black queer aspects of Brooklyn. What I mean by this is that Crown Heights is a neighborhood where two Black men feel comfortable calling each other "baby" ("bae") in a romantic way while in public (even if it is during an argument).

I also had a conversation with Brian—a Black man who is originally from Alabama and works in radio and entertainment in Brooklyn—about gentrification. Brian responded to a request for interviews I sent through an email listserv. When I learned he had moved out of New York City to Jersey City, I asked him, "Do you think you found Jersey City on your own, or do you think gentrification forced you to Jersey City?" He responded by saying,

I don't know. I think you just have to be open. You have to be open for something new. When I first moved here, I wouldn't think to ever go there. If I do go out, I'm going to go to Manhattan. It's just easier to get around. If I get inebriated in public, I feel like I can get a train and go home. If I'm in Brooklyn it would be harder. I know where the trains are, but it would be harder for me to get home. From the shoddy trains for one.

Here Brian does not directly answer my question, but his response leads me to believe that gentrification forced him to Jersey City because of the way he describes being open to the possibility of moving outside of Brooklyn. Perhaps he wants to tell himself this to get him past the experience of moving outside of New York City, and he also does not know whether or not gentrification displaced him. Yet he's right, you have to be open to something new. However, new or renewed public space indicates the reach of gentrification.

According to Summers (2019, 16), "Gentrification is a logic of urban renewal characterized by privatization of formerly public services, multimillion-dollar development projects, physical transformation of spaces, development of new industries, emphasis on the city center, unequal access to the city by the marginalized poor whose homes have been reappropriated to cater to the desires of an elite class of residents and consumers." Gentrification, as Neil Smith (1979, 547) notes, "is the process of converting working class neighborhoods into middle-class neighborhoods through the rehabilitation of a neighborhood's housing stock." Cedric Robinson (2000) argues that capitalism and racism did not break from old tradition, but rather, racism and capitalism fused to highlight the ways in which the Black body is commodified to create what is known as racial capitalism. Gentrification has initial footing in modes of oppression: slavery, colonialism, imperialism, and genocide. These modes of oppression justify capitalism and gentrification and become an essentializing project that illuminates regional, subcultural, and dialectical difference. By essentializing project, I mean the extent to which dominant society will mark and remove people and spaces that do not align with the dominant identity and values.

The dominant identity and values, as I conceive them in my project, are centered on the process of spatial marginalization I call "one-percentification." I introduce one-percentification to highlight a process that speaks to the distinctive, shifting urban landscape of intersecting identities of race, sexuality, and class in Brooklyn. One-percentification is an extreme and widely felt process—at varying registers and intensities—of converting working- and middle-class neighborhoods into solely upper-class neighborhoods. The converting process occurs when (1) corporations begin to take over cityspace, (2) luxury condos begin to line the streets of urban landscapes, and (3) there are affective responses that disturb—or, to put it frankly, hijack—the attunements of the Black queer body in social, nighttime spaces. When these three processes are realized, Black queer people, though displaced, become the real estate upon which dominant society—the one percent in this case—exercises oppression. This process also has an impact on Black LBGTQ public culture considering the closing of Langston's and the displacement of Black LGBTQ people such as Brian. Brian discussed the impact that gentrification has on dating in the Black LGBTQ community, and by extension the lack of Black queer social spaces, because he indicated one particular neighborhood that is supportive of Black LBGTQ people and culture instead of a slate of places:

I feel like you shouldn't have to revert to an online site to meet somebody. I met my boyfriend through work but at the same time it was just a day-to-day natural hi or bye situation. That's the way I would rather it. I don't think it would happen . . . I would never go to an app. Even when you do go to an app, you have to say you are looking for something and you have to find that person who is looking for the same thing . . . it just doesn't work like that. Why is it that we have to always choose online dating? Why is that? Why is it that that is our saving grace is online dating? I mean you have to go to Flatbush. It's a little homophobic but any clubs near Flatbush. I just think it's geared to the community, us.

According to Laam Hae's "Gentrification and Politicization of Nightlife," there is lack of comprehensive national initiatives to promote nightlife or queer social spaces. In Britain, however, nightlife has risen as a policy prerogative (Hae 2011a, 566). The central government in Britain (under the Labor Party of Tony Blair) created deregulatory measures for nightlife businesses (read: queer social spaces) (Hae 2011a, 566). These deregulatory measures extended nightlife operating hours under the Licensing Act of 2003. Yet in the United States, city governments, like that of Brooklyn, New York, struggle over how to contend with queer social spaces and "qualities of life" that rest outside of spaces that rise from heteronormativity. Therefore, various laws have been employed in North American cities, such as Brooklyn, to diminish the nuisance effects of nightlife (see Berkley and Thayer 2000). These various laws are supplemented with broad zero-tolerance policing and quality-of-life initiatives that neoliberalizing cities characterized by one-percentification adopt (Hae 2011a). By highlighting the ways in which important queer social spaces such as the house and Ballroom scene or Kiki scene have been politicized, I hope the understanding of one-percentification, along with the dematerialization—squeezing out—of the house and Ballroom scene, becomes fortified.

Starting in the late 1990s, gentrification in the Lower East Side, Clinton, West Chelsea, Williamsburg, and Dumbo intensified (Hae 2011a, 570). To the local government, dance clubs created nuisance effects, such as publicized incidents of gun violence and drug trafficking, along with other vices. According to Hae (2011a, 570), "a wider range of nightlife businesses, such as bars, lounges, and restaurants, also became main targets of anti-nightlife offensives by residential communities that suffered from these businesses' nuisance effects." Residents of the Lower East Side, Clinton, West Chelsea, Williamsburg, and Dumbo petitioned the State Liquor Authority (SLA) to limit the number of liquor licenses it issued in neighborhoods that are overcrowded with nightlife businesses (Hae 2011a, 570–71). The residents' petition coincided with an influx of wealthier citizens moving into the neighborhood intent on making their neighborhoods a utopia—a utopia necessarily free of queer social spaces and their negative connotations, as well as the queer patrons associated with them. This crackdown on alternative lifestyle businesses, starting in the late 1990s, suggests that New York's house and Ballroom scene or Kiki scene may be dematerialized next.

Loretta Lees (2003) argues that "super-gentrification" is rapidly occurring in Manhattan. Manhattan's "super-gentrification," moreover, involves intense investment and conspicuous consumption by superrich financiers who are products of global finance fortunes and corporations.[1] Neil Smith (2002, 427) contends that gentrification is now a global, urban strategy that is "densely connected into the circuits of global capital and cultural circulation rather than social reproduction." Lees's (2003) "super-gentrification" is a complex process led by state, city, and individual initiatives that support local and national governmental policies. For Lees (2003),

> Not only does "third-wave" gentrification now occur in a variety of sites, but it also takes a myriad of forms. It can be of the *traditional* or *classical* form—that is, by individual gentrifiers renovating old housing through sweat equity or by hiring builders and interior designers and so leading to the embourgeoisement of a neighborhood and the displacement of less wealthy residents. It is now also increasingly *state-led* with national and local governmental policy tied up in supporting gentrification initiatives. (2490)

"Third-wave" gentrification (Hackworth and Smith 2001), "super-gentrification" (Lees 2003), and one-percentification are a matter of unsettled capital supported by a selfish community board that takes over Manhattan's neighborhoods for the sake of creating a heteronormative utopia, or in Michel Foucault's (1986) sense, a "heterotopia." Marlon M. Bailey and Rashad Shabazz (2014) draw from Foucault to demonstrate the ways that heteronormativity influences placemaking. In the next section, I explore care-work in Happiness Lounge based on fieldwork from spring 2019.[2]

---

1. Jason Hackwork and Neil Smith (2001) consider "super-gentrification" to be "third-wave" gentrification. "Third-wave" gentrification occurred in the 1980s in New York, targeting SoHo, NoHo, TriBeCa, the East Village, and the Flat Iron District (Hae 2011a, 570).

2. As of 2023, Happiness Lounge is permanently closed.

Care-Work in Happiness Lounge

Feminist geographers explore care-work as an ethical responsibility that is taken up by society. Feminist geographer Victoria Lawson (2007) raises questions about the role of society in support of cash-poor people, urban decline, unemployment, and vanishing public support for minoritarian people. Lawson (2007, 1) writes, "Care ethics focuses our attention on the social and how it is constructed through unequal power relationships, but it also moves us beyond critique and toward construction of new forms of relationships, institutions, and action that enhance mutuality and well-being." I use care-work in this chapter to explore the ways in which Happiness Lounge becomes a community of care where its patrons are provided with food, family, and affirmative space. Happiness Lounge becomes a community of care through the events that are organized there. For example, the lounge often serves food for the patrons and publicizes patrons' birthdays through a public, physical calendar found on the wall. Also, patrons organize birthday parties for other people that are intimate in scope and feeling. What I mean by this is that the Happiness Lounge becomes a community of care in that the small, cozy lounge places gift tables and creates food areas for the entire lounge to enjoy, as opposed to limiting a birthday celebration to an area or section, table, or patio.

As I enter the lounge, I notice the patrons through the widow. First, a shorter Black man emerges from the rear patio and hurries across an empty, dimly lit secondary space. Two black folding chairs sit empty near the rear patio door. The secondary space is adjacent to the small lounge area. The man carries two large aluminum pans covered with aluminum foil—one on top of the other—with both hands. A small white hand towel hangs from the back pocket of his light denim shorts. He places both pans on top of the bar and a cloud of steam shoots from the foil. He wipes his face with his white hand towel and exits to the rear patio.

"They serving food in here today, sus?" Montae says as he steps into Happiness Lounge. He makes his way past the bar and sits in the empty chair next to me. "It's a chill vibe as usual, right?"

I nod my head in agreement, "Yes."

Furthermore, in my earlier interview with Kenny, he referred to Happiness Lounge as a community of care. In our conversation, he defined a community of care as a dynamic group of people who consciously take care of one another. He remembered a night when he went to Happiness Lounge for his type of self-care: listening to music. "When I would go out, it would be a Black or Latinx club. I think it has a lot to do with music selections. You know what I mean? If you want to go out, have a good time and have a self-care moment, you want to hear great music." Kenny's perspective suggests that Happiness Lounge provides self-care for him considering its "good music," or in other words, its music playlist. The kind of music that provides him with care is the "soca" music that is played in Happiness Lounge. "Soca" is a music genre invented by Lord Shorty (now known as Ras Shorty I) influenced by African and Indian cultures in Trinidad. In an interview, Ras Shorty I said, "Sometimes you have to be bold and just make it plain that nobody else did it. They followed after. I am not the composer of soca. I am the inventor. It's as simple as that. I took out the traditional instruments. I took out the East Indian drum, I take out the dancehall and the mandolin, and I put it on the drum set, triangle, and guitar" (Benjamin 2013).

Considering the history of soca music invented by Lord Shorty, Kenny practices self-care, a form of care-work, by listening to soca music in Happiness Lounge. Self-care is an intentional act to promote individual physical, mental, and emotional well-being. Self-care typologies include listening to and/or playing music, dancing, and more. Furthermore, self-care is a type of care-work that is directed at the self. Considering Kenny's perspective of Happiness Lounge, the space provides patrons with the opportunity to practice self-care in various forms: dance, fellowship with one another, and listening to soca music.

Also, Happiness Lounge is a community of care because of the availability of food and its patrons' knowledge of its availability. In addition, Montae's recognition of Happiness Lounge's "chill" or calm atmosphere is indicative of a space that is conceived from the idea of a place where new social relationships could be created. Taking this further, the availability of food, drink, a dance floor, and the prospect of new social relationships expands the purpose of Happiness Lounge and transcends its identity as a "bar" or lounge—a place where you sit and relax. Happiness Lounge is more than a bar, it a place where Black LGBTQ people can do much more during its open time; it has an expanded purpose. What I mean is that Happiness Lounge is more than a place where you find entertainment for self-care; it is where family is created, maintained, and reproduced.

During another visit in fall 2019, I walk into Happiness Lounge and notice two Black women sitting at the bar. On top of the bar there are three trays. The first tray is filled with red, green, yellow, and purple gobstoppers (a candy). The second tray is filled with cheese crackers, and the third tray is filled with chocolate cupcakes with chocolate icing and sprinkles. One of the Black women at the bar says, "I made these for Zay birthday! We gonna celebrate tuh-night!" The Black women have low-fade haircuts.

Considering one of the patrons brings food to the lounge to celebrate another patron's birthday suggests that the space is more than a lounge; it is a community of care and care ethics that celebrates the lives of Black LBGTQ people. In this regard, Happiness Lounge is a community of care because of the recognition of mutual aid. First, care-work is centered on a feminist care ethic that strives to enhance social well-being. Care-work is, by extension, labor that requires people to connect and establish a relationship centered on support and care for other people. "Care ethics begins with a social ontology of connection: foregrounding social relationships of mutuality and trust, rather than dependence. Care ethics understands all social relations as contextual, partial, attentive, responsive, and responsible" (Horton and Pyer 2017). Next, I will focus on the performance labor in Happiness Lounge.

Performance in Happiness Lounge

Performance is a critical expression filled with intent, language, and stories. I use performance to explain the similar and different everyday practices, movements, and lived experiences in Happiness Lounge. For example, Brian Keith Alexander (2012, 271) says, "performance offers cultural familiars a moment of pause for critical reflection, a meditative moment of comparative experience, sometimes noting same and not the same, further illuminating diversity within community, meaning we're all not the same." Gyptian's remix of "Hold Yuh" featuring Nicki Minaj starts playing from the large black speaker in the corner of the room.

I take a sip of my cocktail, and just as I did during my visits to Langston's, I notice the components of the drink—the prominent taste of whiskey overpowers the taste of cola. I immediately place the cocktail on the silver tabletop, hoping that the ice cubes will dilute the strong, pronounced whiskey taste. In this regard, my taste of a strong cocktail textures the calm atmosphere of Happiness Lounge. Mentally, I recognize the spatial typology of the space; in other words, I mentally index the atmosphere by marking Happiness Lounge as a Black queer spatiality that provides free-poured (nonmeasured) cocktails for everyone's pleasure.

Two Black women immediately stand up near the bar and start intimately dancing to the Jamaican reggae song featuring Nicki Minaj. The first Black woman—a butch femme—wears black pants and a blue and yellow patterned T-shirt. The second Black woman—a high femme—is the same height as the first woman and wears a dress that flows in the wind as she sways her hips from side to side. Her long brown and black braids swing in a direction opposite her hips.

The first woman's long black dreadlocks slightly glide from side to side as she pulls the other woman closer to her body and her right hand explores the woman's neck and moves from her neck to her lower back. The first woman's hand then gently touches the second woman's hips before gliding back up her back. Here, the first woman's touch textures Happiness Lounge's calm atmosphere with moments of desire and intimacy.

Their bodies move on beat to the music. Therefore, their sense of balance is shaped by a dialogic performance; their bodies perform desire that is intimate and suggestive. The women's sense of balance makes Black sexual dissidence more legible through intimate dance while the symbolic heteronormative Blackness of "Hold Yuh" plays. Their sense of balance, then, demonstrates Black queer performativity. Performativity is not a monolithic social operation. Rather, differently placed historical subjects conceptualize the relations between physical bodies and social meanings differently (Manning 2010, 489). On the one hand, their sense of balance engenders queer eroticism, desire, and intimacy, and on the other hand, their sense of balance demonstrates that queer Blackness is already present in Happiness Lounge's systems and practices. This intimate practice is legitimized by systems in Happiness Lounge that are reflected in and protected by Black LGBTQ public culture. Black LGBTQ public culture renders the multiplicity of lived bodies, including these two Black women, as feminine, masculine, queer, intimate, desirable, and so on (Butler 1988; Lott 1993; Rogin 1996). What I mean by these social markers is that gender is an analytic for scholars, a vector of power for people, and a performance for people.

Defining gender requires a consideration of gender in material, discursive, and biologic contexts. In the discursive sense, gender is a regulatory norm, but it is also one that is produced in the service of other kinds of regulation (Butler 2004). By regulation, I mean the ways that language and actions, as two examples, are policed by way of other people, laws, and/or policies. Moreover, regulation stems from the network of power. Power in this sense means that it is diffuse, rather than top-down, unidirectional. Also, gender is a vector of power that serves an organizing principle for social life with material consequences. Specifically, feminist approaches to the sex/gender system highlight what has been taken for granted—gender does not determine sex and sex does not determine gender. Feminist approaches to gender performativity align gender as a vector of power that reconfigures notions of masculinity and femininity that have varying bodily referents.

Back at the birthday celebration, a Black woman sings in the center of Happiness Lounge. The chairs and bar stools are lined against the walls of the bar. A table at the entrance is filled with small gift bags and white and gray balloons. The woman holds the mic and sings "I Have Nothing" by Whitney Houston. Her blond hair shines against the red strobe lights that are circling around the bar. The crowd begins clapping and snapping their fingers. The Black man standing next to me says, "That's it! She did that."

The woman's song performance creates a space where Black LGBTQ people can pause for reflection and see the community's diversity. What I mean by this is that the woman singing requires everyone to stand in a semicircle with the performer at the center. This configuration allows the patrons to literally see each other. In addition, this spatial configuration lends itself to support what Dwight Conquergood calls a dialogic performance (Conquergood and Johnson 2013). The dialogic performance is a practice that allows the audience to engage in a staged moment while seeing the full dynamics and talents of Black LBGTQ public culture, particularly the singing performance and its deep rootedness of Black public culture. For example, call-and-response is a notable practice in Black culture and spaces, such as the church. E. Patrick Johnson and Mag G. Henderson (2005, 144) discuss call-and-response in Marlon Riggs's (1995) documentary, *Black Is . . . Black Ain't*: "The opening of the film with the chantlike call and response of Black folk preaching references a communal cultural site instantly recognizable to many African Americans. But just as the Black church has been a political and social force in the struggle for the racial freedom of its constituents, it has also, to a large extent, occluded sexual freedom for many of its practitioners, namely gays and lesbians." Here Johnson (2005) explores the ways in which Black churchgoers engage in call-and-response during sermons. For example, the preacher will say something and then the audience will respond by clapping or saying "Amen." Over time, the call-and-response practices become louder and more intense. Gays and lesbians are often left out of the call-and-response because they must cover their identities in the name of church.

In addition, Black LGBTQ public culture manifests in Happiness Lounge as DJ Frankie Paradise plays house music. DJ Frankie Paradise is the resident DJ at Happiness Lounge. Fridays are referred to as Frankie Fridays. An older Black gay couple passes by me and one of the men says, "Music pumpin' tonight!" The other man nods his head in agreement. DJ Frankie starts playing "Cape Town" by Sides. The same Black gay couple locks hands and moves to the center of the dance floor. The green and red strobe lights circle the room and move across their bodies. The first man moves his hips from side to side with his shoulders back. The second man nods his head to the beat of the song and then he spins his body from side to side. After two minutes, both men come close together and bend their hips and move low to the ground and back up again. At this moment there is an audience saying, "Ayee!" as most of them begin smiling and clapping to the beat.

The music heard by the people in Happiness Lounge brings the community physically together. The Black gay couple in particular begins to become the focus of everyone's attention—even my own. At the moment when the couple becomes *the* moment, the patrons begin to have a meditative moment of comparative experience on their own. For example, I observe the couple, hear the house music, and feel the beat of the bass below my feet and in my chest. As I sit in Happiness Lounge over time, its sensuous geography comes into focus.

Sensuous geography is a subfield of geography that emerges out of postmodern thought and humanism. Over time, I gain a sense of the space by utilizing sense as both meaning (desire and intimacy are queered) and as feeling or sensation. My sense of spatial meaning is derived from observing and interacting with objects in Happiness Lounge, and then the feelings that I get inside Happiness Lounge make clear the functionality and atmosphere of Happiness Lounge for its users: a Black queer place where Black LGBTQ people can do what they desire to do, within reason. My feelings or sensations, then, clarify social relationships through performances that affect my own feelings. Next, I focus on care-work in Happiness Lounge.

Sus, How Was Your Week?

Bailey (2014) discusses kinship labor while centering Black queer space and Ballroom communities:

> I use the terms *socio-spatial practices* or *labor* to describe the actual work, tasks, and activities that members undertake. Extending Judith Halberstam's (2005) notion of queer space, I define Black queer space as the place-making practices that Black LGBT people undertake to affirm and support their non-normative sexual identities, embodiment, and community values and practices. . . . The gender system defines the roles that members serve in the house. In Ballroom culture, houses are kinship structures that are configured socially rather than biologically. (490, 493)

Therefore, kinship labor is the actual work that people do to create connections to other people; it is the work of producing a kinship structure where people are recognized, affirmed, socially connected to each other. I use kinship labor to demonstrate the ways in which people in Happiness Lounge connect with each other on a familial level to support each other.

"Sus, how was your week?" Montae asks me after taking a sip of his cocktail. Montae refers to me as "sus" (or sister) not because we are biological siblings, but rather to demonstrate a close relationship to me as a member of his chosen family (see Allen 2019).

"It was so-so. I mean it was pretty uneventful. How was your we—?" The bartender's shadow projects onto the wall and my focus turns to her. She stares at Montae with her left hand on her hip, her lips pursed.

Montae starts laughing, "Now, auntie, you know I have been here for a minute and you ain't looked my way."

The bartender looks at me and then back at Montae. She says, "You ain't looked at me! Now give me a hug!"

Montae stands up and wraps his arms around her.

"You need to come over for dinner more often so I can put some meat on them bones you got! When you comin'?"

Montae simply laughs as she turns to walk toward the bar. This moment in the bar represents a labor matrix representative of kinship labor. In this instance, kinship labor is the reciprocal gender and familial norms that are engendered by Montae and the bartender, and their relationship is dialogically volleyed between one another. The kinship labor is not exclusive to this moment, but it is an exercise in and across Happiness Lounge and, as we have previously seen, Langston's. For instance, at Langston's, Aaron called me "sus" and the bouncer called me "brotha" (brother); at Happiness, Montae also refers to me as "sus." These are moments when my emplaced body is interpolated as part of a Black LGBTQ family.

I overhear someone in the lounge yell, "I'll see y'all ladies later!" as the entrance door is opened. I notice two Black women exit. A middle-aged Black man is now coming through door, his head facing two Black women sitting at the long, wooden bar. The Black woman at the left end of the bar wear a navy-blue dress and a pair of white sandals. To her right, a Black woman sits slouched over holding a cocktail in a small, plastic cup. Her long white T-shirt lies bunched at the end of her stool. I walk through the first set of doors and into the foyer. The man tells me, "All right there now, brotha!" The tall Black man wears a tan-colored Kangol hat, a white long-sleeved shirt, dark blue jeans, and brown open-toe sandals. As I pass him, his musky cologne immediately slaps my nose.

When the older man says, "All right there now, brotha!" he means two things. The first thing his words mean is that he recognizes me. His expression is similar to saying, "Hey, how you doing?," an everyday gesture and question between people. Also, the meaning that is attached to his words is kinship by using the term "brotha." Using "brotha" is similar to calling someone "family"—both terms are used frequently in Black vernacular culture (Richardson 2013). Kinship labor is also represented through the recognition of patrons' birthdays.

I stand in front of a long wooden bar. Behind the bar is a Black woman with dreadlocks that hang down her back. She is pulling bottles of vodka from a shelf behind her. At the top of the shelves is a long mirror affixed to the wall. I notice four one-dollar bills taped to the top right corner of the mirror. Bright red string lights hang loosely from each corner of the white ceiling of the bar, drooping low enough to grace the top shelf. To my left, three silver high-top cocktail tables and four tan and black cocktail chairs are scattered along the southern interior wall, where a large June 2019 calendar hangs. As I move closer, I notice several names and initials written on particular days of the large calendar.

The public calendar that is affixed to the wall indicates a familiarity among the patrons and the staff—who are considered family. The names of the people that are written on the calendar is indicative of a kinship structure because an entire calendar is provided for patrons to write in their birthdays so Happiness Lounge can celebrate their birthdays in some way. "Who birthday is it today?" I overhear an older Black man asking the bartender as I walk toward the back of the lounge. Therefore, the birthday calendar is not an aesthetic element in the bar, but a recognized object and a way for everyone to see others' birthdays.

Before the birthday celebration starts, the staff comes in and out of the rear patio door bringing tables, chairs, and balloons into the front area of the lounge. After about fifteen minutes the bartender says, "Hey, brotha, we need to get a tablecloth." The older Black man leaves through the patio and comes back with a white tablecloth to cover the table with.

I watch the two staff members come in and out of the front of the lounge. I ask the Black woman as she speeds past me, "How long have you been working here?"

She stops and turns to me and says, "I think I lost count, but maybe ten years or so. Why you ask?"

With excitement I respond, "Well, I'm just interested to know how long this place has been open and how long you have been here. You seem to know everyone who comes in here." She laughs, and says,

Well, where else can the elders go in this neighborhood? Nowhere like this, I'm sure of it. And I'm Aniya, by the way. I been seeing folks come and go.

Most people in here I grew up with. Some of have kids now, and we have eventually come out to our kids, too. So, the people in here have lived life. You know, there's a woman who comes in here pretty often. Her name is Melissa and she's a divorced older woman maybe in her late fifties or so. She has three children, you know they're grown and all and she wanted to come out to her children as a proud bisexual woman. When she would come in here, we would talk about how she was going to come out to them, tell them her truth you know?"

I nod my head in agreement and ask, "So did she come out to them?"

Yeah, she did, and you know what happened? One of her children, the old-est daughter, stopped speaking to her for about three years. The daughter believed that the divorce was because of who she is attracted to. That was a hard time for her, too. Melissa would come in some days and just sit and cry with me. I would comfort her. You know in our community, we do not talk about parenting as a bisexual mother. We can barely talk about our desire openly either. I mean, as Black women, we are already thought of as loose. She did not know how to handle the situation. But over time, I told her that I would sit down with her and her daughter because I wanted her to reconnect with her daughter and share her feelings. We did, and you know what, they started back talking and they're still working on their relationship to this day.

"Thank you for sharing that with me. Everyone has a story in here like that, probably."

Aniya nods her head in agreement and says, "Well, I gotta get back to set-ting up. I'll be talking to you!" She turns and walks behind the bar to gather more things for the night.

After about forty-five minutes at the lounge, I notice an older Black man walk in wearing an off-white linen suit set. His shiny brown leather sandals shine through the dimly lit lounge. His tall, slender body squeezes past the crowd near the front entrance. He waves to another older Black man in denim shorts and a white tank top. They embrace. Then, the tall, slender Black man sits next to me. I make eye contact with him and he says, "Hey there, how you doing?"

I smile and reply, "I'm doing good. Do you come here often?"

"Yeah," he says, "I come here at least three times a month. You know I usually walk down here from my apartment to watch the game, listen to some damn good singers, and grab some food. This place give it all to you. Plus, it's like a big family here, too. You see the bartender knows all the regulars and asks about your family, your weekend plans, your health if you been in the hospital recently like I was. You get me."

I reply, "Yeah, I get you. In that case, it sounds like people here really see you and care for everyone. What's your name?" He laughs and replies,

I'm James and I been coming here for a long time. I been living in the neighborhood here in Brooklyn for about fifteen years now. I'm originally from the Bronx. Happiness is like my second home. There's so many familiar faces and every time I come in here it's like a family reunion or church with all the people getting up to sing. People can really sing when they snatch that mic. I mean some people get up there and can't hold a note. You better be able to sing up in here, or I will let you know! Frankly, I think it's because we all family in here. It's not like those spots with the young people. We seasoned here and we look out for one another and we love on each other, you know?

I nod and reply, "I can feel the love here. I mean, everyone pretty much knows everyone in here. My friend Montae is making his round hugging everyone he knows." James says,

Yeah, I see him in here from time to time. He's another familiar face. You know you're friends with Montae so you will quickly become family and we will be checking in on you and getting up in your business. It's a good thing, though, don't think it's not. At our age, that's what we do. That's how it's supposed to be. We have to really care for each other. Happiness used to have Frankie Paradise Fridays, too. Whew. I tell you I would be transported back in time.

Montae finishes hugging and speaking to nearly everyone in the lounge and walks up to James and asks, "How you doing, James? I heard you were having some health issues. If there is anything you need, just let me know."

James smiles and points to a shorter Black man in his late fifties wearing a black leather jacket with "United States Marine Corps" on the back. "Lou been spreading my business again."

"You know we have to check on you, James," Montae responds.

"I was just telling your friend here about that," James says. "How we all family in here and we get all in your business. It's funny . . . my business getting spread around now. Montae, as long as I can come in here and get some food, hug on my friends, and listen to some good singing, I will be all right. Besides, the owner gave me a card with some money in it and a fruit basket.

That was nice. I appreciated that, just like I appreciate you. I'll be seeing you around."

James gets up from his chair and makes his way toward Lou. Montae sits down next to me, where James was seated. "This place can get packed, but it's the usual crowd almost all the time."

I respond, "I can tell."

Considering the social relationships, interior objects, and the instances of kinship labor, I recognize a Black queer sense of place in Happiness Lounge. I explore Happiness Lounge's Black queer sense of place in the following section.

Black Queer Sense of Place: Atmosphere, Nostalgia, and Sensation

Atmosphere is the pervading tone or mood of a place; it is an impersonal or transpersonal intensity (Stewart 2011). In addition, atmosphere is almost always changing and becoming, depending on the bodies that are producing the space. Therefore, people's activities in space are restricted by space; space "decides" what actually may occur (Lefebvre 1991). Furthermore, space is marked by its elements and people's activities. Spatial arrangement also decides what actually may occur in space.

The wooden bar inside Happiness Lounge is the activity hub; it stretches ten feet across the space. At 11:23 p.m. one June evening in 2019, there are ten people inside (myself included). I'm seated less than ten feet away from the large bar. Two Black men in their forties are both seated at the table next to me. The first man is wearing red khaki pants and a striped polo shirt. His face rests on his left hand, while his right hand slightly touches the second man's hand resting on the table. The second man is wearing blue khakis and a white polo shirt. Four empty plastic cups are scattered around the small, round tabletop. Their attention is fixed on a sports game that is playing on a television suspended directly above the bar. Although there are two empty tables—one behind me and the other next to the front door—four Black women and two tall Black men sit at the bar, along with a third Black man wearing khaki pants and a green fleece jacket.

"You a mess, Nique! What you havin'? Same thing?" the bartender asks one of the women. She glides to the shelf directly behind her and grabs a large bottle and pours it into a small plastic cup. She finishes the drink off with a dark cola before handing it to the woman.

Happiness Lounge's atmosphere—meaning its tone or mood—is joyous and calm. As I argue in the introduction, spaces are more than settings for human activity; these settings are more than where race, gender, class, and sexuality are realized. Spaces are co-constituted by sensory data including sensation, spatial atmosphere, and nostalgia. Rodaway (1994) states that the sensuous is the experience of the senses. The senses are one of three aspects of Black queer spatiality that give spatial users a clue of a spatial atmosphere that may align with a nostalgic memory. First, the activities, including haptic engagement between people and objects inside of Happiness Lounge, are influenced and tethered by the spatial configuration. According to Ingold (2011, 133), "Haptic engagement is close range and hands on. It is the engagement of a mindful body at work with materials and with the land, 'sewing itself in' to the textures if the world along pathways of sensory involvement." In the front area, secondly, movement and engagement are concentrated and passive. This is due to the limited seating away from the large bar, the availability of seating at the bar, the entertainment above the bar, and the exit/entrance is nearby. Thirdly, the television's low volume sets the maximum speaking volume between people. All three aspects affect sensation and organize sensuous geographies.

Sensation is a physical feeling. The senses are one of three aspects of Black queer spatiality that give spatial users a clue of a spatial atmosphere and nostalgia. In addition, the senses have a level of duality that is often ambiguous. Sensation is asymmetrical to the senses in and of themselves; it is a happening that is activated by a body's visceral acknowledgment.

Sensation provides us with a mental index of a location's atmosphere (its mood or tone). That is, sensation provides a means to attune to a place. In other words, atmosphere is a broad tone of a space and sensation provides structure—to attach meaning to that tone. For example, at 11:58 p.m., Happiness Lounge remains calm; however, the smell of Caribbean food—oxtails, jerk chicken, plantains—permeates the air. Immediately, images of the Nigerian-American Muslim Integrated Community Center are recalled through my mental archive—a collection of memories—because the smell is reminiscent of a suppressed spatial experience; I am thrust back near Claremont and Willoughby Avenues. Therefore, my sense of smell at this time provides depth and understanding to Happiness Lounge; I understand Happiness Lounge as a site where sustenance, particularly Caribbean cuisine, is available to the Black LGBTQ people inside.

Moreover, senses take on two meanings. Rodaway (1994, 4) explains that "the role of the senses in geographical understanding considers the senses both as a relationship to a world and the senses as in themselves a kind of structuring of space and defining of place." The first is sense as making sense; in this form, sense is order and understanding. In this aspect, sense is a mode of meaning. For example, when I first arrived at Happiness Lounge, I recognized that most of the people inside were seated—either conversing with others or viewing a program on the television. I made my way to an empty table to secure a seat. Immediately, I became attuned[3] to Happiness Lounge's calm atmosphere; I got the sense, then, that I needed to have a seat and not disrupt the calm atmosphere of Happiness Lounge. I did not want to cause a scene by standing in the middle of the lounge. The second understanding of sense aligns with a personal feeling or sensation. Sense or collectively, the senses, are the specific sense modes—touch, smell, taste, sight, hearing, and the sense of balance (Rodaway 1994, 5). In addition to the smell and sight of Caribbean cuisine, which are both physical and symbolic codes of Blackness,[4] is the sense of sound. These sensory data, in one way, prompt nostalgia. What I mean by this is that the senses affect memories and nostalgia.

Prompted by sensory data, nostalgia is a sentimental longing or wistful affection for the past. Nostalgia emphasizes the interconnections between body, mind, and place. In this regard, nostalgia is predicated on the entanglement of memory, identity, and place. Place is written on our bodies, wired into our memory. Places become part of us, quite literally. Through place and placemaking, we reify both our individual and our collective identities (Kitson and McHugh 2015). Nostalgia allows us to be thrust back, transported, into the place we recall (Kitson and McHugh 2015). For example, the taste of my strong cocktail emphasizes the interconnections between body, mind, and place. Images of the interior of Langston's rush through my head in an effort to link the present to the past, or perhaps my sense of Happiness Lounge is made clear through mentally archived memories of Langston's that help me to index and attune to the present through the affective atmosphere of Happiness Lounge. In other words, my sensations in Happiness Lounge bring to bear diasporic articulations that are indicative of diasporic LGBTQ public culture.

---

3. Kathleen Stewart (2011) theorizes about attunements using the language and concepts put forth by Martin Heidegger (1962), Thrift (2007), and Sedgwick (1997). Attunements, to paraphrase Stewart (2010), birth dwellings and worldings; attunements are sensed almost always immediately, at various scales.

4. Brandi Summers (2019) discusses how the old "Black" H Street in Washington, DC, was conceptualized as a site of chaos, disorder, and pathology by developers and required the rehabilitation not only of the physical space but also of symbolic codes of Blackness through the lens of a neoliberal project in the purported age of color blindness and postracialism. What manifested is the remaking of Blackness on H Street through Black aesthetic emplacement.

Diasporic LGBTQ public culture includes a set of kinship and performance labor practices and instances of care-work. Considering the squeezing out of Black social spaces across New York as I discussed in previous chapters, diasporic LGBTQ public culture struggles for public space against the backdrop of gentrification.

In addition, the bartender pouring drinks, the chef bringing Caribbean cuisine, and the two Black women dancing, using their hands to explore each other's bodies, are doing types of performance labor. Thus, performance labor is the means by which people make place. Yet care-work involves those mundane and often taken-for-granted moments when a person or people ensure the well-being of another person or group of people. For example, when the bartender suggests that Montae come over for dinner, she does not simply extend a frivolous dinner invitation. The bartender demonstrates a level of care-work that is rooted in a necessity to ensure well-being for Montae.

Conclusion

Black queer people face constant patterns of Black queer spatial extraction across public space. These spaces are fundamental to their joy, care, cultural legacies, and sociocultural futurity because they center their needs. While the production of Black queer spaces is a justice practice, the social dynamics within their interiors help shape and hone approaches to justice and challenge traditional social structures.

Jennifer Susanne Leath's (2023) *Black, Quare, and Then to Where: Theories of Justice and Black Sexual Ethics* discusses "dancing justice." Leath (2023) demonstrates that justice flies and transcends into a cosmic realm, but it is also grounded on earth through dance and performance. Leath (2023) centers both musician Sun Ra and a Black gay, gender-nonconforming millennial, Joseph Lamar:

> Dancing justice with Joseph—holy dancing that presses in, though, and beyond churches—is an unlocking and locking of doors into new dimensions of time and place. Joseph passes between past, present, and future seamlessly. . . . While Sun Ra flies justice into outer space, Joseph is dancing justice on earth. This is to say, Sun Ra is a transcendent figure who invites those who hear and follow him to explore the possibilities of justice that exist in an eternity that is cosmic, not earthbound, connected at once to Saturn (i.e., the planet that is Sun Ra's mother and home, the place through which he is born again) and to ancient Egypt (wherein emphasis is placed

on the eternal life that potentially follows earthly death). To get there, Sun Ra professes his transcendence in terms of his philosophy, work, and sex, one must fly (or transport). One is not dancing into this reality. In contrast, dancing is a grounded, earthbound activity. Through dance, Joseph is connecting material spaces—from his bedroom to the streets to the church to the streets and, eventually, onto the stage. Joseph is dancing justice as he puts together otherwise disjointed rhythms, steps, sounds, and tunes. He is not putting them together for flight, but for dance, for step, for walking into and through—on earth (as it is for Sun Ra in the heavens). The distinction between the flying and dancing of justice must be explained in terms of the difference between a justice that is abstract, postponed, perfect(ed), and ostensibly everlasting, on one hand, and a justice that is concrete/material, now, imperfect(ed), and ostensibly fleeting. These are both ways that justices can do, ways that justicing does. (140–42)

Like Joseph, Black queer people in Happiness Lounge dance as a form of justice. As observed, Black queer men intimately dance with other Black queer men across the space. Their bodies grind on one another as the music plays. Their dance does not consider Western/traditional conceptions of gender and sexuality. Their dance is motivated by their desire to touch and sweat on each other since they cannot dance with each other in public without the chance of violence against them.

CONCLUSION

<hr>

> I feel like I am always going to step in someone dog
> shit or not be around some flavor. I need flavor. . . .
> The feel isn't there. It isn't real. It's got to be real!
> —Brian, 2019

I meet Brian at Junior's Restaurant and Bakery (known colloquially as Junior's) after he's finished work. Junior's is located in Downtown Brooklyn at the corner of Flatbush and DeKalb Avenues. As I get closer to Junior's, I notice three Black men crossing Bond Street. They are cleaning the street and emptying the public recycling and trash bins. A large billboard stands on top of a silver scaffolding. A small poster affixed to the billboard says "RETAIL/ OFFICE SPACE FOR RENT." Across the street from the billboard is a gray building. At the top of the building, a neon sign reads "COOKIES." Several high-rise mixed-use buildings are looming behind the gray building. Two of the buildings are under construction. I notice the juxtaposition between new construction and existing buildings. The street level of the new construction building includes a Chase Bank and retail stores: Express, Forever 21, and Swarovski. Tree canopies line the sidewalks on both sides of the street. An expansive plaza with seating and grass areas characterizes the street opposite the retail stores. I notice the intensity of gentrification, particularly the commercialization of land and curation of nature in society. We sit at a table near the back of the restaurant to avoid the loud noise in the front. I ask Brian about what has changed in Brooklyn since he moved to New York City. Without hesitation, he says,

I saw Brooklyn change. Please believe it. When I first moved to Flatbush, just by the looks of it alone, I didn't see any tall buildings . . . any high-rises. I feel like me coming in and when I actually started living in Brooklyn, it's been a drastic change. It's so drastic. They literally built a high-rise building right across from where I was living. They tore down a boarding house. It was massive. It's kind of like that, you know, that boarding house on *Hey Arnold!* It was like three or four houses. One of the houses is still there at Bedford and Lenox. I guess they didn't buy into the hype. Like they probably had somebody coming to their house asking if they can buy their house. They wasn't havin' that! They literally tore down those houses and built a high-rise. A high-rise! Talk about massive change. It was so much noise all the time. All that banging and you tryin' to sleep.

Brian discusses the ways in which development has impacted his home life in Flatbush, and by extension, his modes of social reproduction. Social reproduction refers to "how we live" (Mitchell et al. 2003). Considering the ways in which a high-rise was built across from Brian's home marks the beginning of gentrification for him. When he discusses the soundscape ("banging" or construction work) that comes with the building, he indicates the extraction of people from a lower tax bracket. In Brian's case, he was squeezed out of the neighborhood. He lives in New Jersey now.

Brian continues discussing the demographic changes in Brooklyn over time while we sit at the center of current construction of green systems, office space, apartments, and retail spaces:

It's [gentrification is] everywhere. I just feel like what is the actual cause of it? I mean I get it, you want to beautify Brooklyn or whatever, but are y'all really trying to push people out, and if so, where are these other people going? Jersey City becoming the same thing. For me, from living there now, and just from me moving people are always saying it was the hood. I was like, really? Yeah, I just want to know the objective. Like I see it in Williamsburg. Like wow, it's very white now. I feel like I am always going to step in someone dog shit or not be around some flavor. I need flavor. They are trying too hard; the feel isn't there. It isn't real. It's got to be real!

My investigation has explored the relationship between displacement, economic deprivation, and spatial marginalization at the interpersonal, institutional, and structural levels and Black queer placemaking practices. *Get Yo' Life: Black Queer Placemaking* has expanded the scope of spatial knowledge to include Black LBGTQ spatial experiences in social spaces throughout the twenty-first century by analyzing sensations, nostalgia, and atmosphere within Starlite, the Warehouse, Club Langston, and Happiness Lounge to understand the ways in which gentrification continues to constrict physical Black queer social spaces and impact the atmospheres and sensations that are unique to them. I introduced Black queer spatiality as the relationship between Black queer placemaking practices and their associated sense experience.

As a research tool used to explain a Black queer sense of place, Black queer spatiality describes Black LGBTQ sensation, nostalgia, and atmospheres, and thereby theorizes its findings by tracing physical spatio-historical processes of extraction to the spatial experiences that are emplaced in Black queer social spaces. *Get Yo' Life: Black Queer Placemaking* has explored placemaking and care-work, as well as gender performance and kinship labor. Particularly, *Get Yo' Life* investigated *how* Black queer people make place and the sensational experiences effected through their practices.

In addition, Black LGBTQ people engage in sociospatial practices to navigate conditions where Black LGBTQ sociospatial life is being squeezed out of public space (McGlotten 2012; Fair 2017; Bailey 2014). Particularly, Marlon M. Bailey (2014) examines the ways Black LGBTQ members of the Ballroom community create Black LGBTQ space to contend with their spatial exclusion from and marginalization within public private space in Detroit. I returned to Brooklyn in 2023 and attended an OTA ball that demonstrated the performance and care-work involved in a ball in New York City. I remember several instances of competitors performing what is known as a death drop. As I previously mentioned, a death drop is the exclamation point on a vogue performance; it is the last move in a vogue performance, which involves the performer spinning, jumping in the air, and finally landing on their back with one leg raised in the air with their toes pointed toward the ceiling. A second performer moved closer to the judges' table so they could observe their crisp, tight vogue movements. Their hands were raised toward the ceiling and their hips moved from side to side. The judges behind the table observed their dance moves while several cameras documented their performance. One of most important features at the ball was a sign raised behind the judges table that reads "HIVStopsWithMe.org." Several health organizations attend balls to provide free condoms and free on-the-spot HIV tests.

In 2020 the novel COVID-19 virus shook the world and brought all in-person events to a standstill, changing the ways that people travel, engage in labor, come together, and make and hold place. At the beginning of 2020, businesses across the United States started paying attention to the ways in which the COVID-19 virus had impacted other regions. By March 2020, people in the United States started paying attention to the deadly impact of the virus.

Businesses started shutting down, the NBA and college leagues suspended their season, schools closed, and streets were empty, but thousands of Americans were already infected. On March 11, 2020, the World Health Organization declared COVID-19 a pandemic (Thebault et al. 2021). As of March 12, 2020, one hundred people in the US had died from COVID-19 compilations, and by December 26 of the same year, the death toll had reached 300,000 (Thebault et al. 2021). Due to mandated stay-at-home orders throughout the year, Ballroom events and gatherings at Happiness Lounge ended. The year 2020 was one in which the world changed as we pivoted to slow the spread of the COVID-19 virus. In July 2021, more than 331 million Americans had been vaccinated to protect against the COVID-19 virus since vaccine administration started on December 14, 2020 (Carlsen 2021). On December 29, 2020, Patricia Cummings, a Black nurse, administered the Moderna COVID-19 vaccine to Vice President Kamala Harris, the first woman of Black and Southeast Asian descent to hold the office of United States Vice President. Vice President Harris received her vaccine on camera to demonstrate to the United States, particularly the Black community, that the vaccine is safe. As a result of the ongoing vaccination campaign, the United States slowly reopened public spaces. Considering the ways in which the COVID-19 virus shuttered many businesses, left many people unemployed, and caused highly anticipated balls and other Black queer events to be canceled across many states, Black queer people have constantly shown resiliency throughout time. While *Get Yo' Life* has featured some Black queer spaces in Brooklyn, my aim is to continue to explore where and how Black queer people make place and also to identify historic Black queer sensations across other boroughs outside of Brooklyn.

REFERENCES

Ahmed, Sara. 2006. "Orientations: Toward a Queer Phenomenology." *GLQ* 12, no. 4 (October): 543–74.

———. 2008. *Queer Phenomenology: Orientations, Objects, Others.* Durham, NC: Duke University Press.

Alexander, Brian. 2012. *The Performative Sustainability of Race.* New York: Peter Lang.

Alexander, M. Jacqui. 2005. *Pedagogies of Crossing: Meditations on Feminism, Sexual Politics, Memory, and the Sacred.* Durham, NC: Duke University Press.

Allen, Samantha. 2019. *Real Queer America: LGBT Stories from Red States.* New York: Little, Brown.

Anderson, Ben. 2009. "Affective Atmospheres." *Emotion, Space and Society* 2, no. 2 (December): 77–81.

Aranda, Elizabeth M. 2003. "Global Care Work and Gendered Constraints: The Case of Puerto Rican Transmigrants." *Gender and Society* 17, no. 4 (August): 609–26.

Armstrong, Elizabeth A., and Suzanna M. Crage. 2006. "Movements and Memory: The Making of the Stonewall Myth." *American Sociological Review* 71, no. 5 (October): 724–51.

Arnett, William, Paul Arnett, Joanne Cubbs, and E. W. Metcalf. 2006. *Gee's Bend: The Architecture of the Quilt.* Atlanta: Tinwood Books.

Arnold, Emily A., and Marlon M. Bailey. 2009. "Constructing Home and Family: How the Ballroom Community Supports African American GLBTQ Youth in the Face of HIV/AIDS." *Journal of Gay and Lesbian Social Services* 21, no. 2–3 (January): 171–88.

Arvin, Maile, Eve Tuck, and Angie Morrill. 2013. "Decolonizing Feminism: Challenging Connections between Settler Colonialism and Heteropatriarchy." *Feminist Formations* 25, no. 1 (April): 8–34.

Attali, Jacques. 1985. *Noise: The Political Economy of Music*. Minneapolis: University of Minnesota Press.

Baderoon, Gabeba. 2011. "'Gender Within Gender': Zanele Muholi's Images of Trans Being and Becoming." *Feminist Studies* 37, no. 2 (June): 390–416.

Bailey, Marlon M. 2013. *Butch Queens up in Pumps: Gender, Performance, and Ballroom Culture in Detroit*. Ann Arbor: University of Michigan Press.

———. 2014. "Engendering Space: Ballroom Culture and the Spatial Practice of Possibility in Detroit." *Gender, Place and Culture* 21, no. 4 (April): 489–507.

Bailey, Marlon M., and Rashad Shabazz. 2014. "Editorial: Gender and Sexual Geographies of Blackness: Anti-Black Heterotopias (Part 1)." *Gender, Place and Culture: A Journal of Feminist Geography* 21, no. 3 (March): 316–21.

Bain, Alison L. and Catherine J. Nash. 2006. "Undressing the Researcher: Feminism, Embodiment and Sexuality at a Queer Bathhouse Event." *Area* 38, no. 1 (March): 99–106.

Baldwin, Davarian L. 2009. "Mapping the Black Metropolis: A Cultural Geography of the Stroll." In *Chicago's New Negroes*, by Baldwin, 27–52. Chapel Hill: University of North Carolina Press.

Bastone, William. 1997. "Quality of (Night) Life Issues." *Village Voice,* March 1997: 1–23.

Beats by Dr. Dre. 2015. "People Aren't Hearing All the Music." https://www.beatsbydre.com/company/aboutus.

Benjamin, Gentle. 2013. *G.B.T.V. CultureShare Archives 1997: Ras Shorty I and Avion Blackman*. YouTube video, 1:14. https://www.youtube.com/watch?v=gpLUUlX39ZE.

Berkley, Blair J., and John R. Thayer. 2000. "Policing Entertainment Districts." *Policing: An International Journal of Police Strategies and Management* 23, no. 4 (January): 466–91.

Berlant, Lauren. 2009. "Affect Is the New Trauma." *Minnesota Review,* no. 71–72 (September): 131–36.

Blake, Aaron. 2023. "Rudy Giuliani's Stunning Fall from Grace, in One Chart." *Washington Post.* https://www.washingtonpost.com/politics/2023/09/05/giuliani-popularity-fall/.

Böhme, Gernot. 1993. *Am Ende des Baconschen Zeitalters: Studien zur Wissenschaftsentwicklung*. Aufl. Frankfurt am Main: Suhrkamp.

Bowden, Kirstie. 2012. "Glimpses through the Gates: Gentrification and the Continuing Histories of the Devon County Pauper Lunatic Asylum." *Housing, Theory, and Society* 29, no. 1 (March): 114–39.

Bowleg, Lisa. 2012. "The Problem with the Phrase *Women and Minorities*: Intersectionality—an Important Theoretical Framework for Public Health." *American Journal of Public Health* 102, no. 7 (July): 1267–73.

Brown, Elsa B. 1992. "'What Has Happened Here': The Politics of Difference in Women's History and Feminist Politics." *Feminist Studies* 18, no. 2 (July): 295–312.

Browne, Kath, and Catherine J. Nash. 2010. *Queer Methods and Methodologies: Intersecting Queer Theories and Social Science Research*. London: Taylor & Francis.

Buckland, Fiona. 2010. *Impossible Dance: Club Culture and Queer World-Making*. Middletown, CT: Wesleyan University Press.

Burgin, Richard. 1998. *Jorge Luis Borges: Conversations*. Jackson: University Press of Mississippi.

Butler, Judith. 1988. "Performative Acts and Gender Constitution: An Essay in Phenomenology and Feminist Theory." *Theatre Journal* 40, no. 4 (December): 519–31.

Butler, Judith. 2004. *Undoing Gender*. New York: Routledge.

Campbell, Courtney J. 2018. "Space, Place and Scale: Human Geography and Spatial History in Past and Present." *Past and Present* 239, no. 1 (May): e23–e45.

Carlsen, Audrey. 2021. "How Is the COVID-19 Vaccination Campaign Going in Your State?" *NPR,* last updated September 5, 2022. https://www.npr.org/sections/health-shots/2021/01/28/960901166/how-is-the-covid-19-vaccination-campaign-going-in-your-state.

Carson, Clayborne, et. al. 1994. *The Papers of Martin Luther King, Jr.* Berkeley: University of California Press.

Casey, Edward. 2000. *Remembering: A Phenomenological Study.* Bloomington: Indiana University Press.

Cavanagh, Sheila L. 2010. *Queering Bathrooms: Gender, Sexuality, and the Hygienic Imagination.* Toronto: University of Toronto Press.

Coe, Cati. 2011. "What Is the Impact of Transnational Migration on Family Life? Women's Comparisons of Internal and International Migration in a Small Town in Ghana." *American Ethnologist* 38, no. 1 (February): 148–63.

Cohen, Cathy J. 2005. "Punks, Bulldaggers, and Welfare Queens." In *Black Queer Studies,* edited by E. Patrick Johnson, 437–65. Durham, NC: Duke University Press.

Conquergood, Dwight. 1985. "Performing as a Moral Act: Ethical Dimensions of the Ethnography of Performance." *Literature in Performance* 5, no. 2 (April): 1–13.

Conquergood, Dwight, and E. Patrick Johnson. 2013. *Cultural Struggles: Performance, Ethnography, Praxis.* Ann Arbor: University of Michigan Press.

Crenshaw, Kimberlé Williams. 1989. "Toward A Race-Conscious Pedagogy in Legal Education." *National Black Law Journal* 11, no. 1 (January): 1–15.

Cresswell, Tim, and Gareth Hoskins. 2008. "Place, Persistence, and Practice: Evaluating Historical Significance at Angel Island, San Francisco, and Maxwell Street, Chicago." *Annals of the Association of American Geographers* 98, no. 2 (June): 392–413.

Crichlow, Wesley E. A. 2004. *Buller Men and Batty Bwoys: Hidden Men in Toronto and Halifax Black Communities.* Toronto: University of Toronto Press.

Dailey, Jessica. 2015. "Brooklyn's Pacific Park Megaproject Just Keeps Growing." *Curbed,* September 22, 2015. https://ny.curbed.com/2015/9/22/9918964/brooklyns-pacific-park-megaproject-just-keeps-growing.

Delany, Samuel R. 1999. *Times Square Red, Times Square Blue.* New York: New York University Press.

Doan, Petra L., and Harrison Higgins. 2011. "The Demise of Queer Space? Resurgent Gentrification and the Assimilation of LGBT Neighborhoods." *Journal of Planning Education and Research* 31, no. 1 (March): 6–25.

Dominus, Susan. 2010. "A Brooklyn Bar and Haven Teeters on the Edge of Extinction." *New York Times,* January 22, 2010. https://www.nytimes.com/2010/01/23/nyregion/23bigcity.html.

Dufrenne, Mikel. 1953. "Phénoménologie de l'expérience esthétique. La notion de personnalité de base et son contexte dans l'anthropologie américaine." In *Revue de métaphysique et de morale* (Paris, France): 432–36.

Durkin, Erin. 2011. "Crown Heights' Shuttered Starlite Lounge to Star in New Documentary." *Daily News,* December 21, 2011. https://www.nydailynews.com/new-york/brooklyn/crown-heights-shuttered-starlite-lounge-star-new-documentary-article-1.994577.

Ellison, Treva. 2016. "The Strangeness of Progress and the Uncertainty of Blackness." In *No Tea, No Shade,* edited by E. Patrick Johnson, 323–45. Durham, NC: Duke University Press.

Eng, David L., Judith Halberstam, and José Esteban Muñoz. 2005. "What's Queer about Queer Studies Now?" *Social Text* 23 (3–4): 1–17.

England, Kim. 1994. "Getting Personal: Reflexivity, Positionality, and Feminist Research." *Professional Geographer* 44, no. 1 (February): 80–89.

Eubanks, Virginia. 2009. "Double-Bound: Putting the Power Back into Participatory Research." *Frontiers* 30, no. 1 (January): 107–37.

Fair, Freda L. 2017. "Surveilling Social Difference: Black Women's 'Alley Work' in Industrializing Minneapolis." *Surveillance and Society* 15, no. 5 (December): 655–75.

Farrar, Margaret E. 2011. "Amnesia, Nostalgia, and the Politics of Place Memory." *Political Research Quarterly* 64, no. 4 (December): 723–35.

FasterCapital. 2023. "Cover Charge Chronicles: What Lies Behind the Entrance Fee." *Faster Capital,* June 24, 2024.

Ferguson, Roderick A. 2004. *Aberrations in Black: Toward a Queer of Color Critique.* Minneapolis: University of Minnesota Press.

Foucault, Michel. 1986. "Of Other Spaces." *Diacritics: A Review of Contemporary Criticism* 16, no. 1: 22–27.

Foucault, Michel. 1990. *The History of Sexuality. Volume 1, An Introduction.* New York: Vintage.

Funes, Maria J. 1998. "Social Responses to Political Violence in the Basque Country." *Journal of Conflict Resolution* 42 no., 4 (August): 493–510.

Gilmore, Ruth Wilson. 2002. "Fatal Couplings of Power and Difference: Notes on Racism and Geography." *The Professional Geographer* 54 (1): 15–24.

Hackworth, Jason, and Neil Smith. 2001. "The Changing State of Gentrification." *Tijdschrift voor economische en sociale geografie* 92 (4): 464–77.

Hae, Laam. 2011a. "Gentrification and Politicization of Nightlife." *Acme: An International E-Journal for Critical Geographies* 11, no. 3 (January): 564–84.

———. 2011b. "Legal Geographies—The Right to Spaces for Social Dancing in New York City: A Question of Urban Rights." *Urban Geography* 32 (1): 129–42.

Harvey, David. 1973. *Social Justice and the City.* Athens, Georgia: University of Georgia Press.

Harvey, David. 1973. *Social Justice and the City.* Athens: University of Georgia Press.

Harvey, David. 1982. *Limits to Capital.* Oxford, UK: Blackwell.

Harvey, David. 1992. "Social Justice, Postmodernism and the City." *International Journal of Urban and Regional Research* 16, no. 4 (December): 588–601.

Harvey, David. 2011. *The Enigma of Capital.* Oxford, UK: Oxford University Press.

Heap, Chad C. 2009. *Slumming: Sexual and Racial Encounters in American Nightlife, 1885–1940.* Chicago: University of Chicago Press.

Heidegger, Martin. 1946. "Letter on Humanism." In *Pathmarks,* edited and translated by William McNeil. Cambridge: Cambridge University Press.

Heidegger, Martin, John Macquarrie, and Edward Robinson. 1962. *Being and Time.* San Francisco: Harper.

Hill Collins, Patricia. 2000. "Gender, Black Feminism, and Black Political Economy." *The Annals of the American Academy of Political and Social Science* 568, no. 1 (March): 41–53.

hooks, bell. 2014. *Ain't I a Woman: Black Women and Feminism.* New York: Taylor and Francis.

Horton, John, and Michelle Pyer. 2017. *Children, Young People and Care.* London: Routledge.

Hubbard, Phil, et al. 2005. *Thinking Geographically: Space, Theory and Contemporary Human Geography.* London: Bloomsbury Publishing.

Ingold, Tim. 2011. *Being Alive: Essays on Movement, Knowledge and Description.* London: Routledge.

Jackson, J. B. 1995. "A Sense of Place, a Sense of Time." *Design Quarterly,* no. 164 (Spring): 24–27.

Johnson, E. Patrick. 1998. "Feeling the Spirit in the Dark: Expanding Notions of the Sacred in the African-American Gay Community." *Callaloo* 21, no. 2 (April): 399–416.

———. 2001. "'Quare' Studies, or (Almost) Everything I Know about Queer Studies I Learned from My Grandmother." *Text and Performance Quarterly* 21, no. 1 (January): 1–25.

Johnson, E. Patrick. 2003. *Appropriating Blackness.* Durham, NC: Duke University Press.

Johnson, E. Patrick, and Mag G. Henderson. 2005. *Black Queer Studies: A Critical Anthology.* Durham, NC: Duke University Press.

Jordan, Jamal. 2019. "'The Energy Was Just Indescribable': Club Langston Didn't Go Quietly." *New York Times,* September 5, 2019. https://www.nytimes.com/2019/09/05/nyregion/club-langston-nyc.html.

Jordenö, Sara. 2016. *Kiki.* Sundance.

Kissine, Mikhail. 2013. *From Utterances to Speech Acts.* Cambridge, UK: Cambridge University Press.

Kitson, Jennifer, and Jonathan Bratt. 2016. "City Sensing and Urban Aesthetics." In *Handbook of Cities and the Environment,* edited by Kevin Archer and Kris Bezdecny, 363–84. Cheltenham, UK: Edward Elgar Publishing.

Kitson, Jennifer, and Kevin McHugh. 2015. "Historic Enchantments—Materializing Nostalgia." *Cultural Geographies* 22, no. 3 (July): 487–508.

Lavers, Michael. 2009. "The Queer Issue: The New Gayborhoods of Fort Greene, Sunset Park, and Jackson Heights." *Village Voice,* June 24, 2009. https://www.villagevoice.com/2009/06/24/the-queer-issue-the-new-gayborhoods-of-fort-greene-sunset-park-and-jackson-heights/.

Lawson, Victoria. 2007. "Geographies of Care and Responsibility." *Annals of the Association of American Geographers* 97, no. 1 (February): 1–11.

Leath, Jennifer Susanne. 2023. *Black, Quare, and Then to Where: Theories of Justice and Black Sexual Ethics.* Durham, NC: Duke University Press.

Lees, Loretta. 2003. "Super-Gentrification." *Urban Studies* 40 (12): 2487–509.

Lefebvre, Henri. 1991. *The Production of Space.* Oxford, UK: Blackwell.

Levy, Nadine. 2016. "Emotional Landscapes; Discomfort in the Field." *Qualitative Research Journal* 16, no. 1 (February): 39–50.

Lorde, Audre. 1984. *Sister Outsider: Essays and Speeches.* Trumansburg, NY: Crossing Press.

Lott, Eric. 1993. *Love and Theft: Blackface Minstrelsy and the American Working Class.* New York: Oxford University Press.

Löw, Martina. 2013. "The City as Experiential Space: The Production of Shared Meaning: The Production of Meaning in the City." *International Journal of Urban and Regional Research* 37, no. 3 (April): 894–908.

Madison, D. Soyini. 2012. *Critical Ethnography: Method, Ethics, and Performance.* Los Angeles: SAGE.

Manalansan, Martin F. 2003. *Global Divas: Filipino Gay Men in the Diaspora.* Durham, NC: Duke University Press.

Manning, Erin. 2010. "Always More Than One: The Collectivity of a Life." *Body and Society* 16, no 1: 117–27.

Marx, Karl. 1978. "The Value-Form." *Capital and Class* 2 (1): 134–50.

McGlotten, Shaka. 2012. "Ordinary Intersections: Speculations on Difference, Justice, and Utopia in Black Queer Life." *Transforming Anthropology* 20, no. 1 (March): 45–66.

———. 2014. "A Brief and Improper Geography of Queerspaces and Sexpublics in Austin, Texas." *Gender, Place and Culture: A Journal of Feminist Geography* 21, no. 4 (October): 471–88.

McGlotten, Shaka, Dána-Ain Davis, and Vanessa Agard-Jones. 2009. "Black Gender and Sexuality: Spatial Articulations." *Souls* 11, no. 3 (September): 225–29.

McHugh, Kevin E. 2009. "Movement, Memory, Landscape: An Excursion in Non-Representational Thought." *GeoJournal* 74, no. 3 (June): 209–18.

McKittrick, Katherine. 2006. *Demonic Grounds: Black Women and the Cartographies of Struggle.* Minneapolis: University of Minnesota Press.

McKittrick, Katherine, and Clyde Woods. 2007. *Black Geographies and the Politics of Place.* Boston: South End Press.

Merleau-Ponty, Maurice. 1964. *Signs.* Evanston, IL: Northwestern University Press.

MIC. 2016. "Ballroom Culture Is about So Much More Than Voguing." YouTube video, 1:10. https://www.youtube.com/watch?v=H7xLt2xHZ4Q.

Mitchell, Katharyne, Sallie A. Marston, and Cindi Katz. 2003. "Introduction: Life's Work: An Introduction, Review and Critique." *Antipode* 35, no. 3 (August): 415–42.

Moss, Pamela. 2002. *Feminist Geography in Practice: Research and Methods.* Oxford, UK: Blackwell Publishers.

Muñoz, José Esteban. 1999. *Disidentifications: Queers of Color and the Performance of Politics.* Minneapolis: University of Minnesota Press.

Nast, Heidi J., and Steve Pile. 1998. *Places through the Body.* New York: Routledge.

New York City Office of Nightlife. September 2019. "Understanding the Cabaret Law Repeal." *NYC Office of Nightlife.*

NYC LGBT Historic Sites Project. 2017. "Starlite Lounge." *NYC LGBT Historic Sites Project.* https://www.nyclgbtsites.org/site/starlite-lounge/.

Oswin, Natalie. 2008. "Critical Geographies and the Uses of Sexuality: Deconstructing Queer Space." *Progress in Human Geography* 32, no. 1 (February): 89–103.

Potts, Patricia. 2013. *Inclusion in the City: Selection, Schooling and Community.* London: Routledge.

Relph, Edward C. 1976. *Place and Placelessness.* London: Pion.

Richardson, Matt. 2013. *The Queer Limit of Black Memory: Black Lesbian Literature and Irresolution.* Columbus: The Ohio State University Press.

Riggs, Marlon. 1995. *Black Is . . . Black Ain't.* New York: Infobase.

———. 2017. "Black Macho Revisited: Reflections of a Snap! Queen." *African American Review* 50, no. 4 (December): 781–86.

Robinson, Cedric J. 2000. *Black Marxism.* Chapel Hill: University of North Carolina Press.

Rodaway, Paul. 1994. *Sensuous Geographies: Body, Sense, and Place.* London: Routledge.

Rodríguez, Juana María. 2014. *Sexual Futures, Queer Gestures, and Other Latina Longings.* New York: NYU Press.

Rogin, Michael. 1996. *Blackface, White Noise: Jewish Immigrants in the Hollywood Melting Pot.* Berkeley: University of California Press.

Rothstein, Richard. 2017. *The Color of Law: A Forgotten History of How Our Government Segregated America.* New York: Liveright.

Rubin, Susan. 2017. *The Quilts of Gee's Bend.* New York: Abrams.

Ruccio, David F. 2014. "Capitalism." In *Keywords for American Cultural Studies.* New York: New York University Press.

Schindler, Paul. 2006. "People of Color Pride Halted at the Boardwalk." *Gay City News,* August 3–9. https://gaycitynews.com/people-of-color-of-color-pride-halted-at-the-boardwalk/.

Sedgwick, Eve Kosofsky. 1997. *Novel Gazing: Queer Readings in Fiction.* Durham, NC: Duke University Press.

Smith, Andrea. 2006. *Colonial Memory and Postcolonial Europe: Maltese Settlers in Algeria and France.* Bloomington: Indiana University Press.

———. 2010. "Queer Theory and Native Studies: The Heteronormativity of Settler Colonialism." *GLQ* 16 (1–2): 41–68.

Smith, Neil. 1979. "Toward a Theory of Gentrification: A Back to the City Movement by Capital, not People." *Journal of American Planning Association* 45 (4): 538–48.

Smith, Neil. 1984. *Uneven Development: Nature, Capital, and the Production of Space.* Hoboken, NJ: Blackwell.

Smith, Neil. 2002. "New Globalism, New Urbanism: Gentrification as Global Urban Strategy." *Antipode* 34 (3): 427–50.

Smith, Neil, and Deirdre Wilson. 1979. *Modern Linguistics: The Results of Chomsky's Revolution.* Bloomington: Indiana University Press.

Soja, Edward W. 2010. *Seeking Spatial Justice.* Minneapolis: University of Minnesota Press.

Somerville, Siobhan. 2000. *Queering the Color Line: Race and the Invention of Homosexuality in American Culture.* Durham, NC: Duke University Press.

Stewart, Kathleen. 2011. "Atmospheric Attunements." *Environment and Planning D: Society and Space* 29, no. 3 (June): 445–53.

Stewart, Susan. 1984. *On Longing: Narratives of the Miniature, the Gigantic, the Souvenir, the Collection.* Baltimore: Johns Hopkins University Press.

Stuart, Ewen. 1984. *Channels of Desire: Mass Images and the Shaping of American Consciousness.* New York: McGraw-Hill.

Suggitt, Connie. 2020. "American Woman Breaks Record for Largest Afro." *Guinness World Records,* December 2, 2020. https://www.guinnessworldrecords.com/news/2020/12/american-woman-breaks-record-for-largest-afro-640715.

Summers, Brandi Thompson. 2019. *Black in Place.* Chapel Hill, NC: UNC Chapel Hill.

Thebault, Reis, Tim Meko, and Junne Alcantara. 2021. "Sorrow and Stamina, Defiance and Despair. It's Been a Year." *Washington Post,* March 11. https://www.washingtonpost.com/nation/interactive/2021/coronavirus-timeline/.

Thomas, Andy. 2017. "Nightclubbing: The Bronx's Warehouse." *Red Bull Music Academy,* March 16, 2017. https://daily.redbullmusicacademy.com/2017/03/nightclubbing-the-warehouse.

Thrift, Nigel. 2002. "The Future of Geography." *Geoforum* 33, no. 3 (August): 291–98.

———. 2007. *Non-Representational Theory: Space, Politics, Affect.* Vol. 3. New York: Routledge.

Urban Areas. 2011. "Crown Heights, Brooklyn (History)." *Urban Areas,* December 1, 2011. https://urbanareas.net/info/resources/neighborhoods-brooklyn/crown-heights-brooklyn-history/.

INDEX

access, 62, 104, 106

accountability, research, 7, 10

aesthetics, 46, 49, 67, 76; aesthetic capacities, 4; aesthetic intensities, 5

affect, 5, 40; in Black queer spaces, 2, 5, 13, 67, 99, 106, 114, 120, 121; and hegemony, 12; and nostalgia, 4, 13, 59–60, 121

Ahmed, Sarah, 66

Alexander, Brian Keith, 111

Anderson, Ben, 4, 59, 65

anti-Black policymaking, 9, 42, 53, 55

anti-Black racism, 33, 40, 46, 49, 70, 77

anti-Blackness, x, 1, 5, 11, 16, 25, 53, 59, 70, 71, 93

appropriation, 46, 47, 91

Appropriating Blackness (Johnson), 24

ArcGIS, 27, 28 figs. 0.3–0.4, 29 fig. 0.5

Atlanta: gentrification in, 58; Midtown, 58

atmosphere, 4, 38, 59, 73, 119–21; in Black queer spaces, 1, 3, 4, 12, 13, 36, 59, 65, 67, 73, 127; of Happiness Lounge, 99, 110, 111–12, 114, 119–21; of Langston's, 62–65, 66; and sensation/nostalgia, 4, 13, 14, 36; of violence, 32

attunements, 121n3

Auburn University, 57

Austin, Texas, 39, 40

Bailey, Marlon, 7, 11, 56, 99. See also *Butch Queens up in Pumps*

Bain, Alison, 11

Baldwin, Davarian, 54

Baldwin, James, 5, 66, 67

Ballroom, 7, 127, 128; community, 15, 16, 127; culture, 15, 16, 55, 56, 64, 98, 100, 107, 108, 114

balls: Apocalypse, 16; OTA, 127; POCC, 78, 80; Uptown Underground, 16

Barclays Center, 13, 14, 32

bathroom, 37, 47, 57, 85

belonging, 9, 64

Berlant, Lauren, 40

Better Days Reunion, 73

Black, Quare, and Then to Where (Leath), 122

Black Belt, 54

Black cultural objects, 46

Black feminism, 7, 8, 10, 11n2

BLACK PERFORMANCE AND CULTURAL CRITICISM

E. PATRICK JOHNSON, SERIES EDITOR
VALERIE LEE, FOUNDING EDITOR EMERITA

The Black Performance and Cultural Criticism series includes monographs that draw on interdisciplinary methods to analyze, critique, and theorize black cultural production. Books in the series take as their object of intellectual inquiry the performances produced on the stage and on the page, stretching the boundaries of both black performance and literary criticism.

www.ingramcontent.com/pod-product-compliance
Lightning Source LLC
Chambersburg PA
CBHW030653270326
41929CB00007B/344